GUIDE ME, HOLY SPIRIT

*God's Divine Leadership
in Your Journey of Faith*

FRANKLIN WALDEN

Unless otherwise indicated, all scripture quotations are taken from the King James Version of the Bible.

GUIDE ME, HOLY SPIRIT
Copyright © 2000

FRANKLIN WALDEN MINISTRIES
P.O. BOX 120
CONYERS, GEORGIA 30012

Printed in the United States of America

ISBN Number: 0-939241-69-2

For Gillie Mae & Sam

I would give anything for one more day with you under the old shade tree. Thank you for your life-long example and the legacy of faith you left to me.

CONTENTS

INTRODUCTION

As I look back over my years of ministry, I know every victory I have won has been because Jesus was right there with me. Every road I have traveled since I was born-again has been a road traveled by the side of my Lord and Savior, Jesus Christ.

As you read this book, I would urge any and all to remember we are nothing without Jesus. We cannot do or accomplish what we need to accomplish unless we are willing to accept Him as Lord of our life and willing to follow the leading of the Comforter, the Holy Spirit.

You can take a trip in a country where you've never been before, but if you don't have a guide, you may never get where you intended to go in the beginning. You could waste many hours, money, or gasoline, trying to find your way around while not knowing anything about the surrounding countryside. If you choose to allow someone to guide you, not only will you avoid the dangers and pitfalls along the journey, but you will get where you wish to go much faster and safer.

The same thing applies in the spirit realm. We can "do our own thing" and not follow the leading of the Holy Spirit. If we do so, we may go to church, tithe, and on the outside look like a Christian. But when Christ returns, instead of saying "Well done, my good and faithful servant," He will look upon us and say,

"...I never knew you: depart from me."

- **MATTHEW 7:23**

I personally would prefer to accept His guidance and enter into His rest. How about you?

1

QUALIFICATIONS
OF A GUIDE

———

While holding a revival in Canada, I met a Brother from Red Lake, Ontario. We became close friends and one day I asked him what kind of work he did. He told me he was a guide. He said, "When people from the United States come to Canada they need a guide. So they hire me for the entire hunting or fishing trip." I asked him what kind of skills one needed to be a good guide. He replied, "Well, you must know a lot about nature and the game you are hunting. You have to understand how each animal thinks. You even need to know their eating habits. A bear has a different nature than an elk or a moose, and likewise, various fish have different natures. You have to be a woodsman and know how to track game and find fish. You have to know the dangers of the wild. You can never be careless. You must be alert at all times. The people you are guiding are totally dependent on you to keep them from getting lost or going the wrong way. They are even dependent on you to help them get the game they are hunting."

Before talking to him, I really had no idea how much responsibility was involved in being a guide. My friend went on to say that if you are a successful guide, people will tip you and tell others how good you are. Their reference would bring more repeat business. But if you were a failure as a guide, no one would use you and you would soon be out of business or perhaps even dead in the wilderness.

When I was just a boy my father was my guide. I would follow him anywhere because I had complete confidence he knew where he was going. My confidence in him took all the fear out of the journey. A few times dad took us "possum hunting" at night. He would lead the way, carrying the lantern that gave the light. I was not afraid because my dad knew the woods and knew where we were going. I trusted him to be my guide.

I loved my dad and as a child, I wanted to be with him all the time. He taught me to respect the elderly and try to help them in any way I could. He said I should love them, and help them make the most of the future they had left. He didn't mean just to help them cross the street or carry a package for them. He meant to help them even when they were in serious need of food, clothing, and shelter.

His advice helped me when I was asked to speak to the elderly in a nursing home one Christmas. I agreed and asked the Holy Spirit to guide me and help me be a blessing to the residents. As I entered the fellowship hall, I saw men and women in all kinds of physical conditions. I realized these people had crossed valleys, climbed mountains, and faced storms I could only imagine and this made me a little nervous. But the Holy Spirit brought to my memory the words of King David in the Psalms.

"I have been young and now am old; yet have I not seen the righteous forsaken, nor his seed begging bread."

- PSALM 37:25

This encouraged me because it let me know my guide was with me. We sang a few songs and then I followed the leading of the Holy Spirit and began to ask them questions about their youth. I started by asking a lady whether she grew up on a farm or in the city. She said she grew up on a farm so I asked if she remembered working on the farm. She began to telling me of all the chores she had to do each day and within thirty minutes I had their attention completely. I reminded them that just as God was with them in their youth, He was still with them today; helping them finish their goal in life and brightening up their future.

When you are young, remember to respect your elders because someday, you too will be elderly with gray and thinning hair. If you will be kind and respectful to your elders, God will bless you. Remember, you reap what you sow. Make sure you sow good deeds and reap God's kindness and not His wrath.

In my lifetime, I have seen hundreds of people who have inherited thousands and thousands of dollars plus houses and land and then wasted it all. They didn't value their inheritance. Although my parents didn't have a lot of money, we valued the thing they left us. They left us an inheritance of faith no one could match. The inheritance my parents left me was to trust God in all things and to believe that when I prayed, God would answer.

My parents had different ideas about raising children than people do today. Dad never took me to ball games and my mom probably never attended a PTA meeting at school. There were no trips to Six Flags and Disney World. The biggest activity we had was getting together on the Fourth of July with our neighbors and having a fish fry and cutting our first watermelon of the year. After we ate, we would play horseshoes or toss washers and the girls would play hopscotch. Then we would have camp meeting.

We would always try to have all the crops tended to before July 4th and then it would be about six weeks before the harvest was ready. During harvest time, mom would can fruits and vegetables to feed us during the wintertime. Those were good times.

When I was growing up, we lived on a farm and there wasn't much money for anything. But my mom and dad both feared God and taught their children to do the same. Dad and mom also taught us certain skills. Although dad was a farmer, he also worked in the cotton mill. Mom ran the house and took care of the family. My dad taught us how to plow the fields for planting the crop, how to raise chickens and hogs, how to milk the cow and many other things we needed to know growing up on the farm. We didn't have an icebox and had never even heard of a refrigerator. We kept our milk and butter cool by putting it in the spring or lowering it into the well in the water bucket. Our evening meal usually consisted of corn bread and buttermilk. Sometimes we would have vegetables and even meat at times. But we always had plenty to eat of whatever was available.

My mother was more like Mary in the Bible in that she was always about the Father's business. But she, too, taught us many things. She taught us not to be wasteful.

We learned a lot about cooking, canning, and other household chores. Although I complained at the time, later in life I came to appreciate what she had taught me.

The most important thing my parents taught me was how to be a disciple of Jesus and how to be led by the Holy Spirit. Faith is an absolute necessity when we are learning to be led by the Holy Spirit. I was very fortunate in that my parents left me a rich legacy of faith. Mom and dad taught by example. They taught me to love Jesus and to love my neighbor as myself. My parents didn't have much formal education but they were educated in the important things of God. My mom would read the Bible by the light of an oil lamp in the evenings before we had electric lights. My dad couldn't even read or write. He'd sign his name with an "X" but he had plenty of good, common sense. He was led by the Holy Spirit every day of his life. My mom and dad were both rich in faith.

As children, we seldom went to the doctor. Instead, my parents used home remedies and prayer to heal us. Dad taught me to have faith in everything pertaining to God. Most of all, he taught me to trust God because nothing was impossible for God.

I remember one year when the boll weevils were destroying the cotton. Dad had done everything he knew to do to stop them and it seemed they just couldn't be stopped. It looked like we wouldn't have a cotton crop that year. One day dad and I walked out in the middle of those nine acres of cotton. Dad took his hoe off his shoulder and leaned on it, bowing his head for just a few minutes. Then he looked up toward heaven and said, "Lord, I've done all I know to do." But then the Holy Spirit spoke to my dad's spirit and he spoke these words as best as I remember them: "I command every boll weevil to leave these fields in the name of Jesus." It was an awesome experience to stand and watch those boll weevils lift and fly off like a dark cloud between us and the sun! Dad made more cotton that year per acre than he ever had before. That's the kind of faith that has been instilled in me and brought me through the many storms in life. And that's a true example of letting the Spirit lead you.

I believe God used my dad to seal the reward of many people during his lifetime.

"He that receiveth you, receiveth me, and he that receiveth me receiveth him that sent me. He that receiveth a prophet in the name of a prophet shall receive a prophet's reward; and he that receiveth a righteous man in the name of a righteous man shall receive a righteous man's reward. And whosoever shall give to drink unto one of these little ones a cup of cold water only in the name of a disciple, verily I say unto you, he shall in no wise lose his reward."

- MATTHEW 10:40-42

I feel this scripture could be used to describe my father. My dad was a true disciple of Jesus and I believe Jesus recognized him as such. I believe every time someone would help my dad, they would seal their reward. I believe this still works today.

Being a disciple means following in Jesus' footsteps and being led by the Holy Spirit. While we may not be great in the eyes of men, we are special in the eyes of our heavenly Father. If we allow Him, God can use us mightily in His service. Then instead of thinking of ourselves as big people, we will acknowledge we have a big God.

The goodness of God and the richness of the faith of my parents have brought more success into my life than I ever dreamed possible. I have never doubted I could cross any valley the Lord chose for me to cross or climb the tallest mountain the Lord chose for me to climb. And I have never doubted I could weather the worst storm of life because of my inheritance of faith in God. I still cherish and hold on to that inheritance today.

My children were not raised like I was. Being a minister, I never had time to do many things with them that I would have liked, but I made sure I taught them about God and about the Holy Spirit as their guide just as my parents had taught me. I've tried to guide my children as my dad guided me. When I go home to be with Jesus, I want to leave them a legacy of faith just like my dad handed down to me.

2

THE
FAMILY OF GOD

After I became a Christian and started on my Christian journey in life, I soon realized I needed someone to help me and guide me in my spiritual walk. My pastor, my dad, and my mom were all much help. But I knew I needed more. It wasn't until I became filled with the Spirit of truth and began to be guided by the Holy Spirit that I could truly understand this Christian walk. This is the reason I feel the Holy Spirit has inspired me to write this book. I want to help others understand.

This book will help born-again people walk closer to God. If you are not born-again, this book will not make any sense to you. A person who is not born-again cannot receive anything from God except forgiveness of sins if he repents. He is a "natural man" and can only receive knowledge through his five senses. He cannot understand the spiritual things of God.

"But the natural man receiveth not the things of the Spirit of God: for they are foolishness unto him: neither can he know

them, because they are spiritually discerned."

- **1 CORINTHIANS 2:14**

There is a natural birth and a spiritual birth. In order to be part of the family of God we must partake of both. The natural man who has not been born-again cannot receive a revelation from God. If he gets a revelation, it will be from the devil. God may speak to him about his soul and bring conviction upon him, but He will not send a revelation to an unsaved person.

Now a natural birth can be understood to a certain degree. But even scientists cannot explain the mystery of birth and how, out of millions of tiny sperm, one certain sperm cell joins with one certain egg cell to produce a child unlike any other child born. They know this joining determines genes for hair and eye color and all the other individual traits that make up each child. But they don't know how the sperm and egg know to join as they do. Isn't it awesome how God even works in a tiny sperm and a tiny egg to bring His will to pass!

Likewise, spiritual birth takes place through God's Holy Spirit. Jesus said,

"No man can come to me, except the Father which hath sent me draw him..."

- **JOHN 6:44a**

When the Father draws us to the Son and we undergo this spiritual re-birth, our nature is completely changed. Before I was born-again, I liked to run with the old crowd in the world. I did things that were wrong because I was not a sanctified person. I smoked cigarettes, I drank alcohol, and I liked to go to dances with the women. But one Sunday morning, standing at the altar, I was born-again. I didn't have any physical manifestations at that time other than tears running down my face but inside I was a different man. My entire nature was greatly changed from that moment forward. Not only did I immediately quit using tobacco and alcohol, God took all the desire for these things out of me. I didn't want to drink, smoke, and go to dances anymore. God had delivered me and taken away all desire for these things.

Some people tell me they have quit smoking but they still have the desire to smoke. This didn't happen with me. When God delivered me, I had no more desire to drink booze, smoke, or run with the old crowd. I didn't want to get on the dance floor with somebody else's wife. I had no desire to backslide into that sin-filled life. My inner man was clean and healthy and my outer man was healed. Praise God, I no longer have a desire to follow the outer man!

I've heard people say, "The devil just won't leave me alone. He's after me, tempting me, day after day." Temptation is a favorite tool of the devil, but there is a way to avoid all temptation. How? We'll deal with this in depth in later chapters.

The Bible says when we put on the nature of Christ, the old nature departs and we become a new creation.

"Therefore if any man be in Christ, he is a new creature: old things are passed away; behold, all things are become new."
- 2 CORINTHIANS 5:17

In other words, when the new nature of Christ Jesus takes over, the old sin nature has to go. We are the family of God and He deals with His family.

"For this cause I bow my knees unto the Father of our Lord Jesus Christ of whom the whole family in heaven and earth is named, That He would grant you, according to the riches of His glory, to be strengthened with might by His Spirit in the inner man."

- **EPHESIANS 3:14-16**

Where did it say God would strengthen us? He strengthens our inner man! Yet most of our religious leaders teach about the outer man, not the inner man. A lot is written in the Bible about the outer man. There are many blessings promised for our outer man, with certain conditions, but God prefers to deal with the inner man. Unless and until we have a knowledge of the inner man, it is not possible to understand the outer man and his reactions. Jesus told His disciples,

"...for out of the abundance of the heart the mouth speaketh."

- **MATTHEW 12:34b**

He was not talking about this fleshly heart that pumps blood through the body, but about the spirit of man, the inner man. What is in the spirit is what the outer man proclaims, professes, and lives. If he has a filthy inner spirit, the man will be filthy. If his spirit is filled with vulgar things such as cursing, swearing, joking, and carrying on, the outer man will act in the same manner. The outer man will act upon the things in the inner man.

What happens when you are born-again and baptized into the family of God? We are baptized into the Body of Christ by the Spirit of the Almighty God. This baptism by the Holy Spirit is what saves and seals us in Him!

We, as ministers, go out and baptize the outer man in water. But it is not baptism in water that saves a man. When I take someone and bury them in that watery grave in the name of the Lord Jesus Christ for the remission of their sins, it is not that act which saves them. It is the baptism that takes place in the inner man through the Holy Spirit that saves and seals us until the day of redemption. I believe in baptism in the name of the Lord Jesus Christ. I do this based on the words the Apostle Paul said;

"For this cause I bow my knees unto the Father of our Lord Jesus Christ, of whom the whole family in heaven and earth is named."

- **EPHESIANS 3:14-15**

Now, if your family name is Smith, then every member of your family is called Smith. Likewise if your family name is Jones, Brown, or some other name, each member of the family goes by that name. So if we are members of the family of God, why would we not go by the name of the Lord Jesus Christ? According to this scripture, Jesus is the one "of whom the whole family in heaven and earth is named."

Paul goes even further.

"Wherefore God also hath highly exalted him, and given him a name which is above every name: That at the name of Jesus

every knee should bow, of things in heaven, and things in earth, and things under the earth."

- PHILIPPIANS 2:9-10

Did he say the name of the Father was exalted above all others names? How about the name of the Holy Spirit? No, he said the name of JESUS was exalted above all other names. The titles of God are Father, Son, and Holy Ghost, as shown in **MATTHEW 28:19**. But the Bible tells us it is in the name of JESUS that all power is given! All believers have one Father and the whole family of heaven and earth is named after that one Father. This is the reason I baptize in the name of Jesus. This is the name above every other name. This is the name of the family of God and everyone who is born-again is a part of this family and shares His name.

There are two steps necessary before we can walk in the will of God. First, we need to accept Jesus as our Savior and be baptized in water in His name. This water baptism acts as a "door" for us to enter into the family of God. This is shown by the words of Jesus.

"I am the door: by me if any man enter in, he shall be saved..."

- JOHN 10:9a

There is also a spiritual being, our inner man, whom God will baptize with His Spirit. When our spirit is baptized into God's Spirit, then our will is subject to His will. This is the second baptism or second step to walking in the will of God.

3

GOD IN CHRIST

——

"For the invisible things of him from the creation of the world are clearly seen, being understood by the things that are made, even his eternal power and Godhead; so that they are without excuse."

- ROMANS 1:20

The spirit world can be understood by the things that are manifested or the things we see. We cannot see the spirit world without a revelation from God, but we can see the resulting life flowing from our inner man. As we look at the human creation of God, we see man is essentially a trinity. He is made up of three parts: body, soul, and spirit. The makeup of man is triune, just like God. After all, man was created in God's image. God is one God, manifested as God the Father, God the Son, and God the Holy Spirit. That's why, after His resurrection, Jesus told His disciples,

"...all power is given me in heaven and in earth."

- MATTHEW 28:18

We must remember God Himself, as the Son Jesus Christ, took on the robe of flesh. He was the fullness of the Godhead that dwelt bodily in the Lord Jesus Christ

(**COLOSSIANS 2:9**). But even though He was in that robe of flesh, He was still the Omnipotent, the all-existing, the all-powerful, and ever-present God. His power and His presence was on earth, and His Spirit was everywhere, including in the man Jesus. His eternal Spirit with all the wisdom and knowledge, and all the understanding and power were resident in the robe of flesh Christ Jesus. However, it did not diminish the headship of the Father.

Jesus was the Son of God because he was begotten of God. He was born of the Spirit due to the overshadowing of the Virgin Mary by the Holy Spirit. The Bible tells us she conceived by the seed created by God the Father. She was used as an incubator to bring forth the manifested Son of God.

Why would God come to earth and become like man? Because in the Garden in Eden, before man could eat from the Tree of Life, the devil got to man and deceived him. Satan injected sin into the picture. So God had to come down to earth as our Kinsman Redeemer so He could restore back what Adam had lost through satan's deception. By this, he not only restored to us the living soul Adam lost, but also the things He intended for the first man Adam to have!

What things are we talking about? Remember, if mankind had not fallen into the temptation of satan and had been allowed to eat from the Tree of Life, he would have been an eternal being; not flesh and blood as we are today. I believe we would have been like we are going to be when Jesus appears; with the body God originally intended us to have.

According to the Bible, Jesus was

"...the brightness of his glory, and the express image of his person."
                                                      - HEBREWS 1:3a

Jesus was the reality of God. He was the real God, in person, expressing Himself to the people. Jesus was the express image of God's substance. Now, just as God was in Christ Jesus when He was here on earth, so is God in each born-again Christian. Jesus was the example of what God wants to be in every one of us. That is God's predestinated plan.

"For whom he did foreknow, he also did predestinate to be conformed to the image of his Son, that he might be the firstborn among many brethren."
                                                      - ROMANS 8:29

I believe every seed, according to the Bible, is predestined to bring forth after it's own kind. Corn was predestined to bring forth corn, birds were predestined to bring forth birds, cows were predestined to bring forth cows, and human beings were predestined to bring forth human beings. This is the way God intended it to be and I don't believe we should interfere with God's plan in any way. If the seed of God, the Spirit, is planted in your heart, you will become a predestined creation of the Holy Spirit. You will be able to grow in the grace and knowledge of Jesus Christ and He will be revealed in you as you grow into the fullness of His stature. If the seed of God remains in your heart, its development will produce a son of God!

"Beloved, now are we the sons of God, and it doth not yet appear what we shall be: but we know that, when he shall appear, we shall be like Him; for we shall see Him as He is."

- 1 JOHN 3:2

The last change, the one that will take place when Jesus returns and we are changed "in a moment, in the twinkling of an eye" is the change that will make us like Him and complete the work satan interfered with in the Garden. Isn't it exciting to know we will one day truly be like God?

4

THE
TRINITY OF MAN

———

In order to continue explaining about the inner being, we need to understand man is a trinity. We have a spirit, soul, and body. In this respect, we are a trinity, yet there is only ONE of each of us. Man has a soul, with the spirit as the center of the inner being, just as the heart is the center of our outer being. Some teach the soul is the mind and some teach otherwise. Whatever you have been taught, you can open up your mind to the things of God and the Spirit of God will teach you the Word of God! Or you can close your mind to the things of God and you will not get anything from the Spirit of God. The choice is yours.

Our mind is like the door to our inner man. We can open the door and have the mind of Christ or close it and refuse to accept the leading of the Spirit. If we have the mind of Christ, we will receive all that the Father has to reveal to us. The Holy Spirit will reveal more truth to us as we continue to grow in His grace through a study of God's Word. But if we close our mind to the leading of the Spirit, because we have allowed intellectual pursuits or the doctrines of man or traditions of man to interfere, then you will find you can't receive anything from the Spirit.

"According as his divine power hath given unto us all things that pertain unto life and godliness, through the knowledge of him that hath called us to glory and virtue: Whereby are given unto us exceeding great and precious promises: that by these ye might be partakers of the divine nature, having escaped the corruption that is in the world through lust. And beside this, giving all diligence, add to your faith virtue; and to virtue knowledge; and to knowledge temperance; and to temperance patience; and to patience godliness; and to godliness brotherly kindness; and to brotherly kindness charity. For if these things be in you, and abound, they make you that ye shall neither be barren nor unfruitful in the knowledge of our Lord Jesus Christ. But he that lacketh these things is blind, and cannot see afar off, and hath forgotten that he was purged from his old sins."

- **2 PETER 1:3-9**

If you fail to do this, then you will be unfruitful in God. You will have the fruit and ideas of man, but you won't have the fruit of the Spirit because you have intentionally cut it off by closing that door. God desires for us to continually refresh our spirit. This is why Jesus could say,

"...that they all may be one; as thou, Father, art in me, and I in thee, that they also may be one in us: the world may believe that thou hast sent me."

- **JOHN 17:21**

He and the Father were and are one in spirit. And where was Jesus before He came to earth?

"In the beginning was the Word, and the Word was with God, and the Word was God. And the Word was made flesh, and dwelt among us...the only begotten of the Father..."
- **JOHN 1:1,14**

"I came forth from the Father, and am come into the world: again, I leave the world, and go to the Father."
- **JOHN 16:28**

God is a Spirit-Being. Through His power, Jesus was conceived in Mary, and God was in Christ as a Spirit-Being. At death, Jesus commended this God-Spirit back into the hands of His Father.

"And when Jesus had cried out with a loud voice, he said, Father, into thy hands I commend my spirit: and having said thus, He gave up the ghost."
- **LUKE 23:46**

Everywhere you go today, people are searching. They may not talk about it, they may not be finding what they need, but each and every one is longing and searching for something. When you repent, searching to be right with God and obedient to Him, man can baptize you in water in the name of the Lord for the remission of your sins. But unless God baptizes your inner man in the Holy Spirit, the work is still not complete. When God baptizes your inner man with the Holy Spirit and comes into your life by faith and grace, then the operation of God starts in you and God's predestinated plan becomes a reality in your life.

I believe every person who is an alcoholic, drug addict, prostitute...all are searching for the missing part of man. I believe they are really searching for God's divine love.

That is the only thing that will fill the empty place in their spirit. Everyone wants to be loved and appreciated. Even God wants to be loved by us and He wants to express His love for us. This is how we worship our Heavenly Father; by expressing our love for Him. Many people think worshipping God is simply a matter of going to church, clapping your hands, or maybe shouting. But when you get right down to it, you worship God in spirit, not in the flesh. When you worship God in the Spirit, you may get emotional sometimes. However, if you are only emotional on the outside without being emotional in the inner man, then your worship is not accepted or in balance with God. It is merely a fleshly reaction.

When your spirit is baptized in the Holy Spirit, your inner man will be in the center of God's Spirit. When the Holy Spirit resides in your spirit, you will have the attributes or fruit of the Spirit.

"But the fruit of the Spirit is love, joy, peace, longsuffering, gentleness, goodness, faith, meekness, temperance: against such there is no law."

                                                                    - **GALATIANS 5:22-23**

The more you grow in Christ, the more you become like Him. Then when Christ returns, our spirit and flesh will be glorified and totally united with God!

5

OUR WARFARE

———

There is warfare going on continually between the flesh and the Spirit. Until we come into the stature of the fullness of the Lord Jesus Christ and the unity of the Spirit, we will have warfare going on in our life. Until we understand there is a warfare going on in our flesh and in our spirit concerning the will of God, we can't understand the spiritual warfare taking place in the world today.

The devil works on the flesh and God works on the inner man. Until we allow the inner man to take complete control and live by the Spirit and not be led by our five senses, this warfare will continue. But when we finally walk in the fullness of Christ and are led by the Spirit in all things, then the warfare will ease off or cease completely. Until that happens, you may not choose to look at evil but you still could hear it. You may not choose to hear it and yet, without thinking, reach out and touch it. You may choose not to touch, feel, hear, or see evil and yet you may taste it. You may choose not to touch, feel, hear, see, or taste evil and yet you may smell it. Without the leading of the Spirit, any one of your five senses could be involved in sin at any time.

But when God, the Holy Spirit, does His complete work in you and me, it won't matter how beautiful it is or how good it smells, tastes, feels or sounds, we will have nothing to do with it. We won't think about or speak evil at any time. And the very idea of being involved in worldly things will be distasteful to us.

I have met very few people who have attained the full stature of Christ. Most of us live too much in the natural man. Many preachers even preach to the natural man. They talk about building their congregation up with the "holy faith." They say they're going to "take the tiger by the tail" and win the world for Jesus. Then satan sends some problem their way and suddenly they're ready to run. They're still in the natural man!

Some people will tell you how good God is and how He brings healing to His people but as soon as the first pain hits, they give up and run to their doctor! That's because they are being led by the flesh and not by the Spirit of God. They are being led by the outer man and not by the inner man of the Spirit. We cannot remain righteous without the leading of the Holy Spirit!

But, you ask, "What IS the inner man?" As we've already discovered, Jesus prayed for His followers,

"...that they all may be one; as thou, Father, art in Me, and I in thee..."

- **JOHN 17:21**

Now Jesus was not asking His Father that His followers be in one accord, although this was necessary. **JESUS WAS ASKING HIS FATHER TO LIVE WITH**

HIM IN THE SPIRIT- BEING OF HIS FOLLOWERS!

How do we know this is what He meant?

"If a man love me, he will keep my words: and my Father will love him, and we will come unto him, and make our abode with him."

- JOHN 14:23

God is not going to abide in our outer being, but He will abide in our born-again, cleansed spirit, which is our inner man!

Under the Mosaic Law, before the Grace Dispensation, God dealt only with the outer man. There was no leading of the Spirit through the inner man. The reason He gave the Israelites so many laws to follow was because the outer man needs someone to lead him constantly.

When we are led through the outer man, we don't take into consideration the condition of the inner man. We may be able to convert the outer man through emotion but if the inner man is spiritually sick, the outer man cannot remain well because the inner man will make the outer man sick again! It is only after receiving the baptism of the Holy Spirit that the inner man can be healed and work with the outer man for true spiritual health. But we must heal the inner man first! When your inner man is baptized into God's Spirit, the same anointing which rested on Jesus will rest upon you and will perfect you. And when the uniting of your spirit and the Holy Spirit takes place and the body is perfected, there won't be any more warfare between the flesh and the Spirit. Both will be led by the Spirit of God and all warfare will cease. I believe this is for us, not just after the resurrection but today!

6

HOW DID
HE DO THAT?

The inner and outer man cannot be in one accord unless they come together as one. The only way they can come together as one is for you to be baptized in and filled with the Holy Spirit. When this happens, the outer man becomes subject to the inner man and you are truly led by the Spirit and not the flesh. Was Jesus filled with the Spirit? Was He baptized in the Holy Ghost?

"Then cometh Jesus from Galilee to Jordan unto John, to be baptized of him...And Jesus, when he was baptized, went up straightway out of the water: and, lo, the heavens were opened unto him, and he saw the Spirit of God descending like a dove, and lighting upon him: and lo a voice from heaven, saying, This is my beloved Son, in whom I am well pleased."
- **MATTHEW 3:13,16-17**

Jesus was baptized in water and immediately He was baptized with the Holy Spirit! This is one of the greatest scenes recorded in the Bible. Here, heaven and earth made a connection. Mercy and truth joined together. Here was a man who, although He was God, took on flesh like a man and reconciled the world unto Himself. He set an example of what we could and should be in this world. He was both God and man, just as every born-again Christian is both God and man. When we are filled with the Holy Spirit, our body is the temple of the living God, just like Jesus. But did Jesus' problems end with baptism? Did satan avoid Him after He was baptized with the Spirit? Does baptism with water and God's Spirit make us immune to temptation from satan?

"Then was Jesus led up of the Spirit into the wilderness to be tempted of the devil."

- **MATTHEW 4:1**

It sounds like Jesus' problems have just begun, right? Here He was in the wilderness. He fasted forty days and forty nights. He was tired and very hungry and along comes satan, the tempter. The first temptation satan brought was one of the flesh. He was tempting the outer man because he found something the outer man needed and desired.

"And when the tempter came to him, he said, If thou be the Son of God, command that these stones be made bread."

- **MATTHEW 4:3**

Satan knew Jesus was hungry. The tempter knew the weakness of the flesh so that's what he attacked first. But Jesus was not only hungry. During this forty day period something else had happened. His Spirit became strong! His will became strong! And notice how Jesus answered the devil.

"But he answered and said, It is written, Man shall not live by bread alone, but by every word that proceedeth out of the mouth of God."

- **MATTHEW 4:4**

Now Jesus could have turned those stones into bread. That was not a problem for the Son of God. But if he had done so, it would have been at the suggestion of satan, and Jesus would have come under the power and will of satan; obedient to the desire of satan!

How did Jesus overcome this temptation? By the Word of God! His answer was preceded by "It is written." Jesus was speaking by the Spirit. This was the Spirit taking over and defending the flesh. He turned from the hunger pains of the natural man and focused on eating from the spiritual table - the Word of God. We see Jesus changed the subject from the outer man to the inner man. It stopped the devil cold! Jesus won the battle by leaning on the Word of God.

Satan had lost the first round so now he began to try something else. He tried to combine the power of suggestion and the scriptures to trick Jesus into proving He was the Son of God. Satan carried Jesus up into the holy city and set Him on a pinnacle of the temple. He wanted Jesus in a high and prominent place in the city. Then, notice satan's challenge to Jesus.

"If thou be the Son of God, cast thyself down: for it is written, He shall give his angels charge concerning thee: and in their

hands they shall bear thee up, lest at any time thou dash thy foot against a stone."

- MATTHEW 4:6

Now this was legitimate scripture satan had quoted. So what was Jesus' reaction to this challenge? How did He answer satan? Once again, Jesus leaned on the inner man, the spirit, and we read,

"Jesus said unto him, It is written again, Thou shalt not tempt the Lord thy God."

- MATTHEW 7:7

Jesus knew satan was telling the truth about the angels. He knew He could call on them for help. But he didn't give in because He knew just what satan was attempting to do. He had been attacked this time in the soul-mind area. Satan had first attacked the flesh. Then he attacked the mind. But Jesus was watchful against the wiles of the devil and detected the evil in his temptation.

Satan was down to his final trick. The Bible tells how satan took Jesus up

"...into an exceedingly high mountain, and sheweth him all the kingdoms of the world, and the glory of them; And saith unto him, All these things will I give thee, if thou wilt fall down and worship me."

- MATTHEW 4:8-9

This time satan was testing the third part of this God-man; His inner man or spirit. Jesus knew the kingdoms of the world had been lost to satan when man fell into sin in the Garden in Eden. He knew they were satan's to give if he chose to do so. He knew satan could bring Him pleasure in the flesh instead of the pain of crucifixion. He knew what He was destined to endure to redeem mankind and the world from sin. In return for what satan offered, all Jesus had to do was fall down and worship satan...just one time! What an accomplishment this would have been for satan if he could have convinced the Son of God Himself to worship him! Did Jesus fall for this trick? Not for a moment. Jesus responded by once again preceding His answer with the words "It is written."

"Then saith Jesus unto him, Get thee hence, satan: for it is written, Thou shalt worship the Lord thy God, and him only shalt thou serve. Then the devil leaveth him, and behold, angels came and ministered unto him."
- **MATTHEW 4:10-11**

Thank God, Jesus won the victory over satan by rejecting all his temptations and by being obedient in the Spirit. He was an overcomer and paved the way for us to overcome also.

Like Jesus, born-again Christians do not have to prove to satan who they are. Satan uses the power of suggestion to tempt us and cause us to fall. Don't ever do anything the devil suggests you to do. Be watchful and alert to any evil that may be in words coming from others and also from any thoughts satan may put into your mind. Our minds are a spiritual battlefield. But all power is ordained of God, including the power satan is permitted by God.

In reality, Jesus defeated the devil at Calvary. We have the power through Jesus' name to defeat him as well, but we have to quit confessing satan's power over us, before we can defeat him. We must reconcile in our mind and spirit that if Jesus defeated the devil at Calvary, he was defeated!

"My people are destroyed for lack of knowledge."
- **HOSEA 4:6a**

People let satan win because they do not understand how the kingdom of God operates. They don't understand the kingdom of satan or where he gets his power. They don't realize satan has no morals. He will take everything he can get and then laugh in your face. He will take advantage of the authority God has given us and destroy us with it through unbelief. We must walk in faith, resisting temptation at every point.

Unless we let the Spirit of God control our life completely and totally, we cannot live a life pleasing to God. That doesn't mean God is rejecting you. It means He is still perfecting you and there is still some work to be done in your life. There is still some surrendering to do. We need to be aware of where we stand with God and what work is being done in our life. If we are not conscious of the work being done on the inner man or what is happening in the outer man, we will yield to the lust of the flesh. After a while, our spirit will be taken over through carnality of the mind and we will give ourselves over to evil works, filthy conversations, and things of that sort.

I believe it is time for us to see the importance of the inner man. When God baptizes us with the Holy Spirit, He does a finished work. But the outer man has not been finished yet. There still has to be a change in him, as we continue putting on the whole armor of God and growing in grace and the knowledge of the Lord. That growth in Christ causes the warfare between the flesh and the Spirit to become weaker and weaker. Temptation becomes easier and easier to resist. As we press forward in faith, there will be a change in the outer man. Come under total subjection to God's Word in every respect and you can be perfected in His love. When you do this, you won't have to worry about the power of temptation because satan will not have any power to tempt you!

For example, when we are oppressed by an eating problem, we need to tell that spirit of gluttony, "I have had enough of that temptation. The Bible says, 'Man shall not live by bread alone but by every word that proceeds out of the mouth of God.' In the name of Jesus, I am going to feed my inner man at least fifteen minutes before I feed my outer man."

This plan will work because you will get so interested in reading and meditating on the Word and have so much joy in learning more truth that you will forget your hunger pains. You will be led by the inner man and not by the outer man.

I had a good friend who was a smoker. He wanted badly to quit smoking and had tried to quit time and time again. But no matter what he tried, it seemed he just couldn't quit. One day he came to me and I prayed with him. Under the anointing of God, the Lord instructed me what to tell him to do. I said, "Brother, you need to go buy a little New Testament. Take the pack of cigarettes out of your shirt pocket and put the New Testament there. Every time you crave to smoke, take the New Testament out and read a

41

verse or two." The man did this and to my knowledge, he has never smoked another cigarette since that day!

We need the Word to avoid temptation. When we are sanctified by the Word it will wash all the habits of sin out! When we are sin-free, our outer man will be controlled at all times by our inner man in regard to all natural desires of the flesh. Instead of the flesh controlling the inner man, the inner man will be in control.

7

VICTORY FOR
THE INNER MAN

The fleshly body has a desire to conform to the world. If you have this problem, the only way to get rid of that desire is to obey the scripture.

"Be not conformed to this world: but be ye transformed by the renewing of your mind, that ye may prove what is that good, and acceptable, and perfect will of God."
- **ROMANS 12:2**

What is the "renewing of your mind?" How do we renew it? We do this by taking on the mind of Christ.

"...let this mind be in you, which was also in Christ Jesus."
- **PHILIPPIANS 2:5**

When we have the mind of Christ we will accept, without question, the things Christ told His disciples. We will be like them...in this world but not of this world.

"I pray not that thou shouldest take them out of the world, but that thou shouldest keep them from the evil. They are not of the

world, even as I am not of the world."

- JOHN 17:15-16

We will be perfected in Christ and will be able to make the same statement Jesus did.

"...for the prince of this world cometh, and hath nothing in me."

- JOHN 14:30b

Satan couldn't find anything of himself in Jesus because Jesus didn't have any unclean or fleshly habits satan could use against Him. Jesus didn't have any attributes of sin in His life but, instead, became sin for us. He took our sins upon himself and died on the cross at Calvary so that we might have eternal life. Jesus not only cleanses sins from our inner man but He also baptizes that inner man with the Holy Ghost, the fire of His Spirit, giving us a pure newborn nature. We are the temple of the living God because the Spirit of God lives in us!

"...for ye are the temple of the living God; as God hath said, I will dwell in them, and walk in them..."

- 2 CORINTHIANS 6:16b

We need to be submitted to God's will. If our spirit is submitted to the will of the Holy Spirit, there is no way, shape, form, or fashion that the devil can break through and touch it. If we have the mind of Christ, we will be in God's will; and as long as we are in God's will, satan cannot touch us without God's permission. He can only go as far as God allows because we belong to Christ Jesus and are joint heirs to the kingdom. We cannot live in the natural if we want to be spiritual. There are people who try to do this but their lives become one-sided and unbalanced. However, we can live in the spiritual and be natural. Our inner man must be healed first and then the natural, or outer man, will be easy to live with and can enjoy the blessings of God.

I have tried to teach my children the importance of living spiritually and putting God's will and Word first in their lives. I feel like they paid attention to my teaching because all of them are active Christians today. One night in Macon, Georgia, I was ministering to the people in a revival meeting. My wife had gone home to take care of some business and my son, Franklin Jr., was sleeping with me. Now for years, I've had the habit of sleeping with my Bible in my arms. We got ready for bed and after we had prayer, Frankie went to sleep right away. When I woke the next morning, he had his arms around the Bible right along with mine.

Sleeping with the Word in my arms keeps me from having nightmares. If anything awakens me in the middle of the night, there is no fear because I have the Word in my arms. I do this, not just because I love the Word but also because it is a type of what I have in my spirit. Jesus taught that the Word and the Spirit were the same. He said,

"...the words that I speak unto you, they are spirit, and they are life."

- **JOHN 6:63b**

Every word in the Bible represents life to a Christian. Who wouldn't want to sleep with their arms around it?

Jesus gave us the secret to a happy and successful life when He was talking to His disciples in the Sermon on the Mount. Here Jesus tells us to

"...seek ye first the kingdom of God, and His righteousness; and all these things shall be added unto you."

- **MATTHEW 6:33**

In this scripture, "kingdom" represents power and "righteousness" represents God's holiness. If we seek God's power and holiness first, He will provide all our needs. We seek His kingdom (power) and His righteousness (holiness) with the inner man, not the outer man. Our inner man should be crying "Abba, Father!" We should be reverent and prayerful while seeking God's kingdom and righteousness. Our inner man must be totally submitted to God, not partially submitted, but totally submitted to Him. Then we won't have to worry about daily needs such as food, clothing, and shelter because God will provide for our needs. To recap, first seek God in power and holiness. Then, we are told

"...my God shall supply all your need according to his riches in glory by Christ Jesus."

- **PHILLIPIANS 4:19**

This is where people get things mixed up. They seek to satisfy the needs of the outer man first, allowing pride or lust to choke out the needs of the inner man. But if the inner man is strong, and we seek God's will first, then all our needs will be met by Him.

46

8

DANGEROUS COUNTERFEITS

―――

With today's technologies, there is a danger of counterfeits. There are counterfeit monies, counterfeit tickets to sporting events, and counterfeit movie passes. There is even a counterfeit to the baptism of the Holy Spirit. We need to beware of counterfeits. I heard someone once say, "God is like Coca-Cola. He's the real thing!" Although I don't exactly like God being compared to a soft drink, He is indeed, the "real thing." We need to remember that for everything God provides, satan attempts to counterfeit.

In the Upper Room, they were sitting there in one accord tarrying for the Holy Spirit.

"Suddenly there came a sound from heaven as of a rushing mighty wind, and it filled all the house where they were sitting. And there appeared unto them cloven tongues like as of fire, and it sat upon each of them. And they were all filled with the Holy Ghost, and began to speak with other tongues, as the Spirit gave them utterance."

- **ACTS 2:2-4**

Where did the scripture say the "rushing, mighty wind" came from? It came out of heaven, causing them to speak in "other tongues as the Spirit gave them utterance." It didn't say they spoke in other tongues according to what someone told them to say. The genuine Holy Ghost comes from God and falls right out of heaven onto you just like it did me the night I was holding hands with two Baptist preachers in an Atlanta revival.

I was a businessman in Atlanta, Georgia and had been taught to fast and pray and tarry for the Spirit. I had done this for months with no result and, in fact, was beginning to think negatively about receiving the Spirit. Of course, the devil was right there to take advantage of this line of thinking but fortunately I had a mom and dad who continued to pray for me daily.

Brother R.W. Shambach, a well-known evangelist, was holding a crusade at Atlanta's Lakewood Fairgrounds. The night I chose to attend the crusade, the Ku Klux Klan chose to burn crosses outside the auditorium. (At that time, blacks and whites were not allowed to sit together in public.) Being a businessman, I just wanted to stay on the sidelines and watch without getting involved one way or another. The newspapers and media were all over the place taking pictures and writing about the scene.

I had been talking to two men from the Baptist church about the Holy Ghost when Brother Shambach began to preach. You could feel the power of God there in the auditorium. Suddenly Brother Shambach stopped and said "Everyone who wants the Holy Ghost, get in line." Now, people began lining up left and right and as each one passed by Brother Shambach, he would lay hands on them and tell them to receive the Holy Ghost. I stood there watching and thinking, "I'm not about to get in that line." I didn't want my picture in the paper. The KKK were still outside burning their crosses. But then I heard a voice whisper softly in my ear, "If you don't get in the line you'll never receive the power of the Holy Ghost." Now I was a dignified businessman and had been preaching for nine months, but when I heard that message in my ear, I broke into a run towards the front of the building. When I stopped, I found myself standing between the two men I had been witnessing to earlier about the Holy Ghost. I remember hearing one of them say, "I thought he already had the Holy Ghost." And that's the last thing I remember!

When I came to myself, I was sitting in the middle of the section reserved for the black Brothers & Sisters and I was speaking in tongues. I was the only white person there and the service was about over. I looked around and said to myself, "I know what I'll do. When Brother Shambach slips out the back way, I will too." Much to my surprise, when the service ended, Brother Shambach and Brother Boyd McClary walked boldly right out the front door, through the KKK. And I was right beside them! I felt ten feet tall and full of the Holy Spirit!

It was some years later before I realized we don't have to tarry for the Holy Spirit anymore. He has already come and has been here since Jesus ascended to the right hand of the Father. All we have to do is surrender and meet the conditions outlined in God's Word. The infilling of the Spirit is ours just by asking. And I have never seen a man or woman the genuine Holy Spirit fell on that has ever backslid. There may be some but I've never met them!

I've seen people get their tongues twisted from somebody whispering in their ears. I've seen people who lived right from Sunday to Wednesday and had to get a re-filling Wednesday night to make it to the next Sunday. Do they think the church is a "filling station?"

"Whosoever drinketh of the water I shall give him shall never thirst; but the water that I shall give him shall be in him a well of water springing up into everlasting life."

- JOHN 4:14

Notice Jesus didn't say you would need to drink again and again to stay satisfied. He said we would have this water within us like "a well of water springing up into everlasting life."

Prosperity is on the minds of people today, because everybody wants to prosper. That's a natural thing to wish for and there's nothing wrong with it as long as you prosper while walking in truth with God. God is not against prosperity.

"Beloved, I wish above all things that thou mayest prosper and be in health, even as thy soul prospereth."

- 3 JOHN 2

Now, if this scripture is taken out of context it can cause much damage in a new Christian's life. In order to get the full meaning of this scripture, we need to read further.

"For I rejoiced greatly, when the brethren came and testified of the truth that is in thee, even as thou walkest in the truth. I have no greater joy than to hear that my children walk in truth."

- 3 JOHN 3-4

There's nothing wrong with wanting to have a nice home, a nice car, nice clothes, and other things. But did you notice in those verses where the emphasis was placed? It was placed on "walking in truth." We've already learned Jesus is the Spirit of Truth and we know we are to walk in His footsteps as closely as we can. So just like the scripture in **MATTHEW 6:33**, we need to keep the Lord first in our life and walk in His truth. Then we can prosper even as He has promised. A gospel of material prosperity without first seeking a spiritual overflowing is a counterfeit of God's true prosperity plan.

The promise of prosperity is not given to those not walking in the truth. But many who do not understand the context of this scripture think they should seek material things. They don't stop to realize they first need to take care of the inner man. When the inner man is in tune with God and walking with Him, then we can ask anything in Jesus' name and have faith we will receive it. God only gives you the desires of your heart when you abide in Him and in His will! We need to remember God's will is His truth and we need to walk in that truth.

As God continues to work on us, we need to work with Him. When we read anything in scripture that God condemns, we need to denounce that thing! We are sanctified by the Word. When the Word condemns something and we believe it and denounce it, right then it is cleaned out of our system. Right then we begin to walk in truth.

All born-again Christians are part of the family of God. Just as in our fleshly families, older children can have influence over younger ones. Mature Christians can often have great influence over those who have just been converted. Be careful your influence is good and that you teach these newly converted ones to walk in truth. Seek God, be holy, live holy, and act holy and you won't lead anyone wrong when they come into the family of God.

We need to be perfected in God and reverently worship in Spirit and truth. Beware of being only a show of the flesh. When we have a problem and don't know what to do, we need to stop and meditate on what Jesus would do in that same situation. If we reject the fleshly suggestion and counterfeit of satan and turn to the inner man, He will reveal to the outer man what to do. But if our outer man decides what we should do without first counseling with the inner man, we can get into serious trouble because we will be walking away from the truth and not in it!

9

GOD WITH MAN
AND GOD IN MAN

Our bodies are temples of the Living God.

*"For He dwelleth with you, and shall be in you...If a man love
me, he will keep my words, and my Father will love him, and
we will come unto him, and make our abode with him."*
- **JOHN 14:17,23**

If we are walking in truth and in the will of God, then God
dwells in us and with us at all times. It is God working
through us that makes a difference. We should not want,
nor believe we deserve, the honor or glory for what we do.
Instead, we need to remember "to God be the glory!" God
does not share His glory with anyone. When we feel
important in God, no self-pride is involved. We are free to
glorify God in all situations and boast all we want as long as
we are boasting in Christ Jesus and not in ourselves. Notice
again the wording of the scripture where the Apostle Paul
prayed,

*"...that he would grant you, according to the riches of his glory,
to be strengthened with might by his Spirit in the inner man."*
- **EPHESIANS 3:16**

But what is the inner man like? Is it a vapor of smoke? Is it a ghost-like substance? Let me tell you what God showed me about this subject. The experience I am about to relate to you really happened. It wasn't a vision, dream, or my imagination. It was the way God chose to reveal more about the spirit world to me. Read carefully and know I will not lie. I fear God too much to do that.

We had been conducting a tent meeting in Bradenton, Florida years ago. I had just come home to the little apartment where my wife and I were staying during the revival. Carolyn was in the kitchen fixing something to eat. The afternoon had been hot and we had had a tremendous service but I was tired. I went to lie down on our bed to rest while she fixed the meal. While lying on the bed, I left my body! I came out of my fleshly body, stood up, and looked back at myself lying there on the bed.

This was not a vision or a dream. When I finish describing this, you will realize it will be a pleasure when your time comes to leave this world. It will be a pleasure because you can do what Jacob did and we read about in **GENESIS 49:1-33**. You can draw your feet up on the bed, smile at everyone, and say "I will see you on the other side."

I stood there looking at myself lying on the bed and suddenly realized I had never had so much freedom. It seemed I had been in prison and had just been released. I was still filled with the Holy Spirit, but somehow I was freer than I had ever been before. I was as conscious out of my body as I had been in it. I could see, hear, think, and I knew just as much as I did before I left my body. I realized it is truly the Spirit that gives us knowledge in this body.

There were jalousie windows in our door and my spirit was just standing there by the door, ready to go somewhere. Then someone came and knocked on the door. While I stood there (in the spirit), I had to make a decision. I had to decide whether to let them find my dead body on the bed and watch them take me off to the undertakers, or whether to go back into my body. I decided to go back into my body and got up and invited the person at the door into the apartment. This is a true experience. I was a form...a spirit-body. I was not vapor, not smoke, and not some ghostly matter but a spirit form. When you understand the reality of the spirit realm, then death loses its sting. You begin to realize we don't really die at all. We just move from one place to another.

One other thing I have learned is the inner man, (or the spirit), must feed on spiritual things in order to stay healthy. We all know the outer man needs to eat the right kinds of food in order to stay healthy but people forget the inner man needs the right kind of food, also. If you eat a doctrine that is not truth doctrine, it will cause you to become spiritually sick in your inner man just as eating the wrong foods will make you physically sick in your outer man.

I knew a fellow once who didn't eat right and he kept getting sicker and sicker. I tried to tell him a lot of his problem was he just ate too much. This man could eat a whole pot of spaghetti at one time. It wasn't so much what he ate as it was how much! I was trying to explain he was getting too much starch in his system. But he had the wrong attitude because he would say "Well, bless God, if it makes me sick, it just makes me sick. I'm still going to eat it."

This is the attitude many people have toward eating the wrong spiritual food. They will go to church and "eat" any doctrine or teaching because it sounds pleasing. They hear a good sounding prophecy and some shouting and the flesh is entertained. A good example of this is when someone told me "I went to a meeting and I know the preacher wasn't right, but we sure had a hand-clapping, foot-stomping service. He didn't preach the right doctrine, but the Spirit of God was there." This is typical of so many people. Instead of judging spiritual food from a spiritual viewpoint, they judge it from a fleshly viewpoint. Our spirit cannot be healthy if we gobble down everything that comes along; accepting the doctrinal teaching of man as truth, when in fact it may even be unscriptural. You might say you will just take the good and leave the bad.

"...Know ye not that a little leaven leaveneth the whole lump?"
- 1 CORINTHIANS 5:6b

If we meditate on the untrue, it can settle in our long-term memory or subconscious mind, allowing for deception through the "knowledge of good and evil."

In the Old Testament, the manna in the wilderness was for the natural man. Jesus, the Bread of Life, is for the spiritual man. If the blood is the life of the natural man and our body is the temple of the Holy Spirit, then obviously the Spirit is the life of the spiritual man. Jesus said,
"...the words that I speak unto you, they are spirit and they are life."
- JOHN 6:63

Jesus is referred to in **JOHN 1:1** as the "Word" and here He tells us His words are life and spirit to us. If we look at this from a spiritual viewpoint, we can see in reality our life comes from the Word of God and from the Spirit of God.

"In the beginning was the Word, and the Word was with God, and the Word was God. And the Word was made flesh, and dwelt among us..."

- JOHN 1:1,14

Jesus was the Word made flesh and He dwelt among us. His words were spirit and life. Therefore we need to feed the inner man just as we do the outer man.

"Your fathers did eat manna in the wilderness, and are dead. This is the bread...that a man may eat thereof, and not die. I am the living bread which came down from heaven: if any man eat of this bread, he shall live forever: and the bread that I give is my flesh, which I will give for the life of the world."

- JOHN 6:49-51

Jesus knew the majority of the multitudes that followed Him did so for the physical food He provided. So He gave them an example to follow in John chapter 6. If we put His words into modern English we find He was, in effect, saying "Okay, you want to feed the old man Adam all the time with the fishes and loaves. You follow Me just for that because that is all you see in Me. You know when you get hungry I can multiply the fishes and the loaves. But that is not the bread you should desire. You should desire food for the inner man - something that can give you eternal life. Don't desire something that will just sustain the body for a short time but something that will give you life forevermore. You should desire to drink the water of life that will quench your thirst, so you will never thirst again."

Many people do not understand what Jesus was talking about when He spoke of bread that would make you live forever and water that would quench your thirst so well, you would never thirst again. That's because they are operating in their five-sense knowledge instead of in the Spirit. Remember earlier when we talked about how people who were not born-again could not understand spiritual things?

The water of life (the Holy Spirit) is like an artesian well. It never runs dry. Jesus told His followers,

"He that believeth on Me...out of his belly shall flow rivers of living water. This spake He of the Spirit, which they that believe on Him should receive..."

- **JOHN 7:38-39**

The Spirit is to well up in us like a river and flow out to other people. But it has a hard time flowing when there is warfare with the flesh. We need to be as careful of the inner man as we are of the outer man. Then we'll be spiritually healthy and in "good shape."

10

THE QUICKENING SPIRIT

"And so it is written, The first man Adam was made a living soul; the last Adam was made a quickening spirit. Howbeit that was not first which is spiritual, but that which is natural; and afterward that which is spiritual. The first man is of the earth, earthy: the second man is the Lord from heaven. And as we have borne the image of the earthy, we shall also bear the image of the heavenly."

- 1 CORINTHIANS 15:45-47,49

The Apostle Paul tells us there is a natural body and a spiritual body. He says the first man Adam was a living soul with a natural body. The "second man Adam" (Christ Jesus) was a quickening Spirit. The natural body is flesh after the earth. The spiritual body is Spirit after the heavens. I believe this pure, spiritual inner being, born-again of the Spirit, is the one spoken into existence by God. I believe it has been cleansed and is no longer defiled by the lust of the flesh. It is a spiritual body!

Someone once asked me what the term "a virgin Christian" meant. This term refers to a Christian who is not tied up, bound, or defiled in any way with the system of man. There is no conflict between this Christian and God or between the flesh and the Spirit. If you are under the domineering power of man; if you are involved in a cult, sect, or religious order where you are required to be more subject to that order or it's leaders than you are to God, then there is a conflict in your relationship with God. If this is the case, you cannot be considered a virgin Christian because your flesh and your Spirit are in warfare.

Now don't misunderstand; it isn't that I object to people fellowshipping in the Word and I don't have a problem with Bible Studies, Sunday School, etc. I do have a problem with people allowing the outer man to control the inner man. It isn't supposed to be that way. When we let the inner man control the outer man then we are in a place where we can receive from God. We are in the will of God and our inner man is a quickening Spirit. It's hard to understand how this works, just as it is hard to comprehend how the body works the way it does. Even medical science doesn't understand the entire make-up of the body of man. After millions of autopsies, they still don't understand the complexities of the body's operation.

In their research, they have found something that has baffled all scientific understanding. We have two brains. Arguably, some of us don't even use one of them but we do actually have two! Right between both brains is a little gland about the size of a garden pea. It is called a "pineal body" and no one knows what it does or why it is there. Medical science has been unable to identify its purpose. But I believe it is a "receiver" to the spirit man. I believe what happens when you have a vision is that both brains operate as one.

I heard the story of a certain atheist who conducted tests on people who were dying. This atheist wanted to know what, if any, difference there was in death between a person who did not profess Christianity and the person who had been "born-again." So he hooked up an electrical monitoring device to a dying Spirit-filled woman and when she died with joy in her heart, the needle jumped, registering enough power to send signals from one radio station to another, all across the earth with some left over!

They hooked the exact same device to a man who did not even believe in God, who was cursing and swearing as he died. The needle went in the opposite direction as far as it could go. When the atheist saw the results, he declared, "Now I understand how these people can stand in their church or home and offer up a simple prayer and talk to God somewhere in the universe and get an answer back." The man sought God and was saved!

That's why I believe that little pea-size pineal gland is a spiritual "computer-receiver." When we receive after the flesh, we receive fleshly things, but God wants us to be tuned in to the Spirit so we can receive spiritual things also. Let me give you an example of being "tuned in" to God.

I set aside a special time every afternoon for Bible study and prayer. I do this in order to prevent my time from being taken up with many other things. During this time I prepare myself to deliver the message God lays on my heart. Some years ago, during a revival, a certain Brother came to me each night after the service and asked, "What time today did you get the text for this message?" Every night of that revival, it turned out God gave the same text to each of us at exactly the same time in totally different locations! After this experience, I began to think how people could receive the same message from the same television channel at the same time. All they have to do is tune in! Likewise, if the church (the body of Christ) is tuned in spiritually to God, then God can reveal the mysteries of Christ to each inner man at the same time. When this revelation gets to the inner man, the outer man will express what is on the inside and will speak only that which is in the Spirit.

"For out of the abundance of the heart the mouth speaketh. A good man out of the good treasure of the heart bringeth forth good things: and an evil man out of the evil treasure bringeth forth evil things."

- **MATTHEW 12:34-35**

The heart is the spiritual center of man. All the knowledge you have is somewhere in your heart. If a man is filthy in spirit, his heart will be filled with filthy knowledge and he will speak filthy things. However, if he is clean and righteous in the spirit, he will speak clean and righteous things. The words are there but they are spirit. They run through the mind, across the voice box, and are spoken but then the words of thought become spirit again. The inner man is then quickened by the Spirit of God. When you, as a born-again Christian, speak the Word of God under the anointing from the inner man, knowing God is in you controlling your speech, then whatever you speak from the Spirit is the same as "thus saith the Lord." When the inner and outer man are in one accord, Christ can use us as an instrument to minister to other people who are hurting.

11

THE AUTHORITY OF THE HOLY SPIRIT

———

The Word of God tells us God is the Head of Christ, just as Christ is the head of man, and man is the head of woman. We need to understand Christ is the head of the inner man. He is head of all of His family. When we walk in the Spirit of God, then our words, communications, conversation, and our conduct will all be in accord with the headship and mind of Christ and will reflect the fruits of the spirit. They will be holy since they will be coming from a holy God.

Let's look back over what we've already learned. If our attention is on the outer man, and we are trying to make sure it has all the comforts of life, we have missed the message the Spirit is sending us. We don't comprehend the fact that no matter what material things we have, if God doesn't come first in our life, we have failed our inner man. There's nothing wrong with material possessions and comfort as long as you keep God first in your life. But we need to learn to be content wherever we are.

Next, it's important to keep the inner man healthy and the only way to do this is to keep him in God's Word. We must continually talk to that inner man. We must study God's Word and pray without ceasing so we can strengthen and feed our inner man. There have been times when I prayed all night. I will wake up and start praying, hold my Bible in my arms, quote scripture and meditate on them. I want to always keep my mind on the Lord.

"Thou wilt keep him in perfect peace, whose mind is stayed on thee: because he trusteth in thee."

- **ISAIAH 26:3**

We need to keep our inner man healthy just as we need to keep our outer man healthy. If a disease gets into our body, then death is in our body because sickness is a type of death. If it stays in our body, eventually it will kill us. For example, if you get a liver disease and you don't get it healed or cured, it will finally kill the liver and you will die. The health of the inner man affects the health of the outer man. If the inner man gets sick, then a spirit of infirmity, a deaf spirit, or some other spirit can get into your body and cause it to become sick and diseased. These spirits need to be cast out of your body, not out of your spirit. A spirit needs a body to operate from before it can do its damage. A Spirit-filled person cannot be possessed by any of these evil spirits but they can be oppressed by them.

Now the next lesson to learn is to be sure of God's timing when operating in the Spirit. We can jump ahead of God the same as we can fail to act upon His Word. To be in one accord, our intellect, the natural mind, must agree with the spiritual mind. We have to get the flesh and spirit in one accord in order to do spiritual things.

I've had to learn to wait on God. There were times when I would pray for someone and say 'Bless God, the Bible said it, now be healed in Jesus' name,' and nothing would happen. It was because I missed God's timing. I tried to jump ahead of Him. Once I went with a Brother to pray for a paralyzed man who had lay helpless in bed for three months. I got very excited when his wife told me about a dream she had, where I prayed for him and he was healed. I said to her, "Let's go and get this job done." I prayed for the man but nothing happened. He still couldn't move. I couldn't understand what had happened. I sat down, prayed, and waited on God. The Lord showed me I had jumped ahead of His timing. I had gotten into the flesh instead of weighing things out in the Spirit.

I analyzed the dream this man's wife had shared with me. In the dream, she saw me, another Brother, and her neighbor present in the room when her husband was prayed for and healed. As the Spirit quickened this to me, the door opened and the neighbor came in; just like in the woman's dream. Instantly the anointing came upon me. I went into a vision and saw his condition, prayed the prayer of faith, and that afternoon he was out in the field on his tractor; healed by the power of God!

This experience taught me to wait on God and let Him do His work through me. I have to wait for His leadership. I learned not to let the flesh get ahead of what the Spirit was telling me to do but instead be guided by the Spirit. I learned the thoughts of the outer man quench the anointing of the inner man every time! But if you can get them working together, whatever you say, and doubt not in your heart, shall come to pass.

Several years ago, we were having a tent revival in Moultrie, Georgia. There were warnings of a tornado coming through Fort Valley heading straight toward Moultrie! I was standing with my brother Howard near the tent just as the service had started. I looked up and here came that funnel toward us, roaring like a freight train. I got under the tent but didn't say anything because I didn't want people to panic. Instead, I walked across the platform and started leading them in singing "There is Power In The Blood." Knowing the tornado could strike at any moment, I still wanted to praise the Lord. Suddenly, as we were singing, the Lord spoke to my inner man and said, "You have power over that storm." I raised my hand, moved the microphone away from my mouth and said, "Peace, be still." My brother Howard told me later he had been watching the funnel cloud and when it came within one hundred fifty yards from the tent, it suddenly turned and went through the woods like a giant bulldozer. It tore down tobacco crops, barns, towns, and woods doing millions of dollars worth of damage. But it never even touched us or the tent! All the while the tornado was wrecking havoc and destruction, the tent was standing and people were still singing "There is Power in the Blood." Now, you can't do that in the natural man!

I want you to understand we have to gain victory in this warfare between the flesh and the Spirit. We have to get the inner man and the outer man coordinated with each other. Then we will be able to face satan and win in the strength of the Spirit of God!

Unless we think in the Spirit, our thinking can be wrong. My wife asked me one day why I never worry. I told her there was no need to worry when you have faith in God. Many of you worry about your job; thinking you might get fired or the company might go bankrupt. But when you have faith in God and are led by the inner man, then you work for a "company" that will never go bankrupt. You take directions from the Most High God of all creation. When you understand all this, you can be a powerhouse for God!

Many people don't even know what it means to operate in the name of Jesus. There is power in that name. Remember what Peter said at the Gate of Beautiful?

"And a certain man lame from his mother's womb was carried, whom they laid daily at the gate of the temple which is called Beautiful, to ask alms of them that entered the temple. Who seeing Peter and John about to go into the temple asked an alms. And Peter, fastening his eyes upon him with John, said, Look on us. And he gave heed unto them expecting to receive something of them. Then Peter said, Silver and gold have I none; but such as I have give I thee: In the name of Jesus Christ of Nazareth rise up and walk...he leaping up stood, and walked, and entered with them into the temple, walking and leaping and praising God."

- **ACTS 3:1-8**

Just look at the power in the name of Jesus! The man had been lame from birth but, in the name of Jesus, he began walking and leaping and praising God. That's why I try to do everything in the name of Jesus. All power is in His name and it is there that we are renewed in our spirit.

67

The inner man has no age! He never grows old! When you are born-again and baptized in the Spirit, the inner man is already in eternity. Your joy is in the inner man. Now I'm not talking about joy as in laughing at something someone tells you. That is a soulish, fleshly joy. There's nothing wrong with having joy in the flesh but we need the joy of the Lord in our inner man to keep us strong. Otherwise, we may find ourselves focusing attention on the cares of this life and the things of the flesh instead of focusing on the spiritual side of things. Our focus needs to be on the things of God, not the things of the flesh. If we are not careful, satan will beat us down in the flesh so we are ineffective in the Spirit. To keep this from happening, you need to follow the scriptural admonition.

"Submit yourselves therefore to God. Resist the devil, and he will flee from you. Draw nigh to God, and he will draw nigh to you."

- JAMES 4:7-8a

If we resist satan and draw nigh to God we will be overcomers and anything we ask, in Jesus' name, will be ours.

"And we are his witnesses of these things; and so is also the Holy Ghost, whom God hath given to them that obey Him."

- ACTS 5:32

The Holy Spirit is given to those who obey God. Therefore, we must feed the inner man with the Word more than we feed the outer man. Never doubt that demonic powers are out there just waiting for you to stumble or weaken. Fallen angels and other spirits, under the leadership of satan, are at work throughout the country in every major city and state. They stir up crime and sin. We cannot control crime because we don't have that power in the natural. But we can protect ourselves from thieves and criminals of the underworld in the natural. To do this we need to know something about the underworld that is against us in the spirit realm. We need to know something about how satan and his demon hordes work. God has given born-again Christians all the power and protection we need to overcome satan and his demons. He has filled us with the Holy Spirit and has angels encamped around and about us. But it is up to us to use the help He has provided.

Once there was a problem with a Brother that affected my Evangelistic Board of Directors. One of the board members came to me and suggested we deal with it according to the Bible. I agreed and we asked another of my board members to draw up a legal contract just as if we were buying a piece of property. He wrote up a contract for us and when written out in proper form it read: "We, the undersigned, do agree thus...and thus...and thus...and the adversary and the conspiracy against us cannot proceed any farther than it has. It will never rise up against us any more, for

"...if two of you shall agree on earth as touching anything that they shall ask, it shall be done for them of my Father which is in heaven."
- **MATTHEW 18:19**

We placed this into a written contract and completed it as a lawyer would with our signatures at the bottom confirming what we had agreed upon. I took a copy and each board member took a copy. We wanted to be prepared so when we needed it, we could just pull out our contract, read it over again and say, "This is our agreement." It's easy to agree with someone in the outer man but when we have an agreement in the inner man, we find a spiritual bond is formed that will stand the test of any circumstance.

Many people have lost the vision of the operation of God in man, and are feeding and enjoying the blessings of the outer man. They are failing to be the good stewards they should regarding their inner man.

God is coming back for His Church. When He does, the outer man will be changed but the inner man should already be changed. The inner man should be made pure when we are born-again and filled with the Holy Spirit. We need to dwell on eternal things and the only thing eternal about us is our inner man. If we concentrate on the outer man we will perish but if we concentrate on the inner man we will find everlasting life. God will never let you down if you seek His righteousness and holiness first!

We need to be sure we have the fruits of the Spirit and not the fruits of this world, so we will be known as sons of God. When we are born-again, the only part of us that can fear is our flesh. The Spirit dwelling in the inner man does not fear. That's why satan comes against us through the outer man; to try and make us afraid. We need to face satan through our inner man and remind him we are not afraid.

"For God hath not given us the spirit of fear; but of power, and of love, and of a sound mind."

- 2 TIMOTHY 1:7

12

KING OF
THE CASTLE

———

"There was a man of the Pharisees, named Nicodemus, a ruler of the Jews: The same came to Jesus by night, and said unto him, Rabbi, we know that thou art a teacher come from God: for no man can do these miracles that thou doest, except God be with him. Jesus answered and said to him, Verily, verily, I say unto thee, Except a man be born again, he cannot see the kingdom of God. Nicodemus saith unto him, How can a man be born when he is old? ...Jesus answered...Except a man be born of water and of the Spirit, he cannot enter the kingdom of God. That which is born of the flesh is flesh; and that which is born of the Spirit is spirit...Ye must be born again."

- **JOHN 3:1-7**

When we are born again, the Holy Spirit indwells us. He will be our Comforter and our Strength. We may not be as strong in our body as those who lift weights but we will be strong in the Spirit and that's what's important! Keep your spiritual muscles exercised and strong because you are not in a flesh and blood struggle. We are entangled in spiritual warfare! It is a warfare of truth against error, a warfare of right against wrong! We cannot ride the fence because there is no middle ground. We are either standing with Jesus Christ against satan or we are deceived by the devil and in danger of eternal destruction! We must not let anyone or anything deceive us. We are commissioned to be strong witnesses of the revelation of Jesus Christ!

"Who shall separate us from the love of Christ? Shall tribulation, or distress, or persecution, or famine, or nakedness, or peril, or sword? Nay, in all these things we are more than conquerors through him that loved us. For I am persuaded, that neither death, nor life, nor angels, nor principalities, nor powers, nor things present, nor things to come, Nor height, nor depth, nor any other creature, shall be able to separate us from the love of God, which is in Christ Jesus our Lord."
- **ROMANS 8:35,37-39**

I had a charismatic Brother, a good friend of mine, come to me one day and try to convince me a person could be demon-possessed and still have the Holy Spirit. He was a very intelligent man. He had a doctorate degree, a Ph.D., and other degrees from various colleges. After he had spent four hours trying to convince me, I said, "Brother, I admire you, but do you mean to tell me that with all your degrees you are this ignorant? Are you seriously telling me a man who is filled and sealed with the Holy Spirit of promise according to **EPHESIANS 1:13**, who has the mind of Christ and demonstrates the fruit of the Holy Spirit, can be demon-possessed? Is that what you're trying to tell me?" He thought a moment and then dropped his head and said, "No, when you put it that way, I guess not."

Friends, that's the only way you can put it! When you are filled with the Holy Spirit and have the mind of Christ, it is impossible for the devil to possess you!

Over my years of ministry I have learned satan can and does oppress and attack the body of man. I have learned he can even cause a demon spirit to possess one who is not born-again. But I do not believe the spirit of a born-again person can be possessed by a demon spirit. I believe an individual can be harassed by demons. I even believe they can be oppressed by demons if they allow him, by not exercising their God-given authority. **BUT THEY CANNOT BE POSSESSED BY DEMONS BECAUSE THE SPIRIT OF A BORN-AGAIN PERSON BELONGS TO GOD AND SATAN HAS NO RIGHT TO GOD'S POSSESSION!**

When Jesus Christ is Lord of your eyes, your ears, your smell, your taste, and your touch, the devil cannot possess you! God did not make man a duplex so the devil could dwell in one part of him and God in the other.

Being a member of a church or regular church attendance won't guarantee you are born-again. I know church members who try to serve God with their five senses but have never been born-again. They live off the experiences of other people. That's how some churches draw large congregations of unsaved people. They find one person who has had a marvelous experience with God, or someone who has a great testimony, and they use this person's testimony to attract unsaved people who live by their five senses. Now I don't see anything wrong with a church attracting unsaved people this way as long as their motives are to help these unsaved become born-again. They need to remember the unsaved need to be saturated in agapé love. Where there is agapé love, in the church or the home or in one's life, there will not be confusion, fighting, or division. Everything God does for His children, He does because He loves us. Likewise, what we do for the unsaved should be because we love them with the same kind of agapé love.

It's this love that will lead us into the marvelous light of God's Word and allow the Holy Spirit to guide us from sense knowledge to spiritual knowledge in the wisdom and understanding of God. Before He went away, Jesus promised that He would send us a helper to instruct, reprove, and help us enter the stature of the fullness of Christ Jesus.

"Nevertheless, I tell you the truth; It is expedient for you that I go away: for if I do not go away, the Comforter will not come unto you; but if I depart, I will send him unto you... he will reprove the world of sin, and of righteousness, and of judgment... when he, the Spirit of truth, is come, he will guide you into all truth: for he shall not speak of himself; but whatsoever he shall hear, that shall he speak and he will shew you things to come..."
- JOHN 16:7-15

The Holy Spirit will teach us to be overcomers. But we will never be overcomers in the battle of life as long as we continue to live in five-sense knowledge. We must realize our battle is spiritual and we must put on the whole armor of God before we can fight in the spirit realm. This can only be done when our spirit has been recreated, or born-again.

Man cannot be the success God has intended for him to be when he relies on his five senses. He will only accomplish in life what he can see, hear, feel, smell and taste. He will be like Thomas who didn't believe until he could touch Jesus' hands and feet where the nail holes were and put his hand into Jesus' riven side. Thomas only believed

what he could see and until he physically saw Jesus with the
holes in His hands and feet and side, he didn't believe Jesus
was risen. Let's look at the account.

*"But Thomas...was not with them when Jesus came: The other
disciples said to him, We have seen the Lord. But he said unto
them, Except I shall see in his hands the print of the nails and
...thrust my hand into his side, I will not believe. And after
eight days again his disciples were within, and Thomas with
them: then came Jesus, the doors being shut, and stood in the
midst, and said, Peace be unto you. Then saith he to Thomas,
Reach hither thy finger, and behold my hands; and reach hither
thy hand, and thrust it into my side: and be not faithless but
believing. And Thomas answered and said unto him, My Lord
and My God. Jesus saith unto him, Thomas, because thou hast
seen me, thou hast believed: blessed are they that have not seen,
and yet have believed."*

- JOHN 20:24-29

We should not be doubters like Thomas and require
proof before we follow the leading of the Holy Spirit. It is
the Holy Spirit who will lead you into all truth. Jesus is the
light and there is no darkness in Him. It is important we
walk in the light and fellowship of Jesus. Paul tells us,

"Be ye not unequally yoked together with unbelievers..."

- 2 CORINTHIANS 6:14

This scripture doesn't just apply to marriage; it
applies to all aspects of life. A person filled with the Holy
Spirit will walk in the light because they walk with God.
They will have a perfect relationship with the Father and
the Son. They will always seek the Father's will. On the
other hand, an unsaved person will seek the fleshly things

of life and walk in spiritual darkness because the darkness hides their sinful deeds. But we, as sons of God, must walk in the light of God's Word. We need to remember if we are believers, we will be moved by God's love to please Him in everything we do. We will be eager to do as Jesus did and follow His example in order to please God. If we cannot follow in Jesus' footprints and walk where he walked regarding spiritual matters, then we are not worthy of being called "joint heirs with Christ" or "sons of God".

"And he that taketh not his cross, and followeth after me, is not worthy of me."

- **MATTHEW 10:38**

How do we take up the cross of Jesus? We do this by being willing to deny ourselves regarding earthly or fleshly things. We do this by being willing to give up control of our life to do the things Jesus commanded His followers to do. We do this by putting God first in our lives above all others, including our parents, mates, children, friends or other relatives — even above our own wants and desires. Jesus did not say we must give up father, mother, brother, sister, etc. But He did say we must be willing to give them up for His sake, if they interfere with our doing God's will.

The Holy Spirit will never lead us to act upon God's Word with the intention of drawing attention to ourselves or bringing glory to anyone other than our Heavenly Father. Even the Holy Spirit never speaks of Himself but will always speak of Christ when He is revealing truth to a new Christian.

"But when the Comforter is come, whom I will send unto you from the Father, even the Spirit of truth, which proceedeth from the Father, he shall testify of me."

- **JOHN 15:26**

At the time we were born-again, a measure of faith was given to us so we could please God by acting on His Word. The Holy Spirit will always encourage us to use this faith to serve God knowing that doing so will please the Father and bring His will to pass in our lives. Being obedient to God brings many blessings we otherwise would miss. One of these is

"If ye shall ask anything in my name, I will do it."

- **JOHN 14:14**

I know, without a shadow of a doubt, if you are a born-again Christian and you have faith, this promise will be true in your life. This does not mean your every wish will be instantly fulfilled. But it does mean that as long as what you ask for is in line with God's will, you will be blessed with it.

If we are sons of God, we won't need to draw attention to ourselves or impress anyone with our faith because they will see it demonstrated in our lives. We will be able to walk with God as Enoch did and have a testimony pleasing to God. Let's take on the nature, love, and the righteousness of God our Heavenly Father. Then we will have the ability to stand in the Father's presence without having any sense of guilt, inferiority, or condemnation. Then we will truly understand righteousness as God views it.

It takes more than faith to make us perfect or righteous now. It takes the wisdom of God. It takes abiding in His agapé love and walking in it each and every day if we are to continue toward perfection in Christ Jesus. If we step out of God's agapé love, we leave the place of safety He has chosen for us. But if we abide in His love we will have life and have it more abundantly. Jesus' mission statement is,

"...I am come that they might have life, and that they might have it more abundantly."
- **JOHN 10:10**

We should examine ourselves daily to be sure we are abiding in agapé love. It is important to walk in faith and in the light of God's Word because when we step out of the light, we step into the darkness where satan rules. There we begin to live in the realm of our five-sense knowledge. There we begin to live in a state of sin consciousness.

Before you can be saved or healed of your sickness, you must be convinced in your spirit that God laid that sin or disease on Jesus. If God laid it on Jesus, and you accept Jesus' substitute as your own, then your sins are remitted and you stand before God as though sin had never touched you. The same laws hold true in regard to diseases. Many diseases are spiritual problems manifested in a physical body. Often when spiritual healing comes, physical healing is right behind. We need to reconcile our physical and spiritual bodies. We must first guard our spiritual health and then we will be healthy physically as well.

And we should never doubt God's Word or His promises. None of His words are void of fulfillment. He watches over His Word to make it good because He is a defender of our faith. If God promises you something, you can be assured He can and will produce it. He does not lie and He does not change His mind.

"For ever, O LORD, thy word is settled in heaven."
                                                    - **PSALM 119:89**

One day, while reading this scripture, the Holy Spirit showed me God's Word must also be settled in my heart. I don't need to try to settle it again; I just need to accept it as being settled and established, knowing the Word of God is not void of fulfillment. I am no longer afraid to act upon God's Word because I know it is true and I confess this truth to all who will listen. When we believe God's Word is settled in heaven, it is because the Spirit of truth has taught us not to doubt God's Word but to always believe it. This allows it to be settled in our hearts. When this Word is fulfilled in our heart, we will bind an accuser on earth and they will be bound in heaven. We will find whatsoever we say will be done just as Jesus said it would and all we have to do is keep God's commandments. We will know our heart needn't have any fear because the Most High God is our friend.

A man's faith and joy are measured by his confession. And the extent to which we confess Christ as our wisdom is the extent to which we will have God's wisdom. We should make this confession continually in everything we do in life. We should never forget to thank God for His wisdom. I thank God daily for His wisdom in this manner: "I thank thee, Father, that you make Jesus' wisdom available unto me. I know as I walk in fellowship with the Word today, your wisdom will be mine in every crisis. Amen."

God will respond favorably to us if we act upon His Word in total faith. Then we must act upon that faith in the name of Jesus. We can say we believe God's Word, but if we never act upon that Word, our faith is dead. We will not be able to please God because it is impossible to please God with faith that is dead and inactive.

"But without faith it is impossible to please him: for he that cometh to God must believe that he is, and that he is a rewarder of them that diligently seek him."

- **HEBREWS 11:6**

"For as the body without the spirit is dead, so faith without works is dead also."

- **JAMES 2:26**

The Holy Spirit has taught me the finished work of faith in a Christian's life should be the desire to rule with Christ during the thousand years of His millennial reign on earth. If we strive for this goal as we walk through our earthly journey, we will please the Father by letting Him have His way in our lives.

13

THE LEADING
OF THE HOLY SPIRIT

———

We were given the Holy Spirit to lead us back to God so we could fellowship with Him as Father and son. He also gave it to us to be our teacher and guide. In John, Jesus told us the Holy Spirit (or the Spirit of truth) would take the Word of God and reveal the Father to us through it.

"Howbeit when he, the Spirit of truth, is come, he will guide you into all truth...whatsoever he shall hear, that shall he speak: and he will shew you things to come."

- **JOHN 16:13**

The Holy Spirit will guide us from one depth of truth to another until we come into the stature of the fullness of Christ. Then we will have a relationship with the Father like Jesus had while He was on earth. We can walk in that relationship until the time we go to live with the Father in the place Jesus has gone to prepare for us in heaven. This is just one "truth" the Holy Spirit guides us into. The Holy Spirit will reveal to us how the Father and the Son came and took up their abode with us. He will show us how special we are to God.

"What? know ye not that your body is the temple of the Holy Ghost which is in you, which ye have of God, and ye are not your own? For ye are bought with a price: therefore glorify God in your body, and in your spirit, which are God's."
- **1 CORINTHIANS 6:19-20**

Just imagine, our body is the temple of the very Spirit of God. God is a Spirit and the Holy Spirit guides us into God's righteousness where we can take on His very nature. Then the Holy Spirit brings us into God's wisdom so we can understand the mysteries of God. This is a very special kind of fellowship we've been invited into. When we have this kind of fellowship with the Father through the Holy Spirit, then the Son will see us in the same way He saw those disciples He chose to follow Him while He was here on earth. He will then intercede and pray for us just as He prayed for His disciples;

"...Holy Father, keep through thine own name those whom thou hast given me, that they may be one, as we are."
- **JOHN 17:11**

Once we allow the Holy Spirit to lead us, we will be set free from bondage of self, fear, poverty, and other things in the natural realm. God's love casts fear aside. When this is revealed to us, we soar like an eagle in the spirit realm and our faith will never die again. With the help of the Holy Spirit, there is no reason we cannot live a victorious life. So, if we are living in defeat, we should listen to what the Word says.

"Greater is he that is in you, than he that is in the world."

- 1 JOHN 4:4

Then we can remind satan, "in all these things we are more than conquerors through him that loved us." Why are we "more than conquerors?" Because Jesus conquered it all for us and all we have to do is accept the reward. We need to stop running from satan and run toward him with the sword of the spirit in our hand and clothed in the armor of God. We need to confess our faith, stand on the Word of God, and we will find the devil is defeated in our life.

Jesus gave us the promise He would "never leave us or forsake us" and we can stand on that promise. God is faithful to His promises. His Word does not return to Him void but it always accomplishes whatever He sent it out to do. This doesn't mean we will never face another storm or never have to climb another mountain. It just means He will be with us when we need Him.

Personally, there have been many times I have faced storms in life and even walked through the valley of the shadow of death. But I was never alone. Like King David, I found Jesus to be my rod and my staff. He's my Comforter who leads me beside still waters. He walks with me and makes my cup to run over with His blessings. When we meet the conditions of the Word of God, there are no promises He has made to His children that He will not fulfill. His Word says He will not withhold any good thing or any perfect gift from His children (**PSALM 84:11**). He does this because He cares for us. All we have to do to receive this promise is to love the Lord with all our heart, mind, and soul, and love our neighbor as ourselves.

GUIDE ME, HOLY SPIRIT

When we take on the mind of Christ, our thoughts will be pure before Him.

"Unto the pure all things are pure..."
- **TITUS 1:15a**

When Jesus was teaching His disciples on the side of the mountain He said,

"Blessed are the pure in heart: for they shall see God."
- **MATTHEW 5:8**

The majority of Christians believe this means we shall see God when we get to heaven. However, if we will just let the Holy Spirit teach us, we will understand this means we will see God "in action" through His mighty power, defending our faith while we are still here on earth!

God is still in charge of all His creation. Understand that when God speaks, His Word is not void of power or fulfillment. But it is impossible to serve God with only our five senses because we cannot always trust what we see, hear, smell, taste, or touch. Our five senses may lie to us and make us believe things are something they are not. It is not in our secular intelligence that the Holy Spirit teaches us but in our born-again spirit. It is here where we can find God's wisdom, nature, righteousness, and holiness.

Having the righteousness of God means you not only stand before God without guilt but also that you can stand before the devil without fear. Having the holiness of God means you are living a life that is pure in every area. This cannot be done by trusting in five-sense knowledge but it can be done by trusting God. When we have a recreated spirit, God's divine love will flow through us as it did from the heart of Jesus our Lord. The Holy Spirit will be with us at all times to reveal the perfect will of God in our everyday life as well as in our future. In this way, He can help us make the right decisions. He will show us who Jesus was when He was with the Father before the foundation of the world. He will show us the glory Jesus had and teach us of the love the Father had for Jesus before He gave Him to die on the cross for us.

We will be able to look into the heart of God and see the kind of love it took to sacrifice the life of His only begotten Son for the sins of others. We will see the love Jesus had, to be willing to lay down His life for our sins. Then we will love like Jesus did with true agapé love. We will have compassion on poor suffering humanity just as Jesus did. In other words, we will be like Him!

As we become more like Jesus, the Holy Spirit reveals to us what Jesus told His disciples.

"Ye shall receive power, after the Holy Ghost is come upon you: and ye shall be witnesses unto me both in Jerusalem and in all Judea, and in Samaria and unto the uttermost part of the earth."
                                                                    - **ACTS 1:8**

This anointing is for all who believe. It is for all who will totally surrender to the call of the Master. The Holy Spirit will reveal to each one how the Father and Son are one and how they and the Holy Spirit are one. Then He will reveal to us how they live in our body as the temple of the Holy Ghost. When we are filled with the Holy Spirit and guided by His presence, we will never again question God's wisdom or knowledge but instead the Holy Spirit will help us to understand it.

Jesus said, "I am the truth." Then He went on to say to know the truth would set us free of satan's bondage. The Holy Spirit teaches us truth is not a thing but is actually the person of Christ Jesus. Another reference to Jesus as "truth" is found in where the psalmist writes,

"Mercy and truth are met together; righteousness and peace have kissed each other. Truth shall spring out of the earth; and righteousness shall look down from heaven."
- **PSALM 85:10-11**

Day by day as we continue our walk with God, the Holy Spirit reveals more about the person Who is truth to us. He will always uphold Jesus and teach us how to be more like Him. When the Holy Spirit reveals this to us, we have no problem acting upon the Word of God in faith. This self-same Spirit, the Spirit of truth, is the same Spirit bearing witness to a believer that the Father and Son are one. It is the same Spirit that reveals to us Jesus is the "Word" and also that He is the Son of God. This is the truth that the Holy Spirit gives to the believer in order to bring him into the true person of Jesus Christ. Truth can only come to a believer from the Holy Spirit through Jesus who is the "door". Why is Jesus called a "door?" Because only through Him can we gain entrance to eternal life with our Heavenly Father.

"Verily, verily I say unto you, He that entereth not by the door into the sheepfold, but climbeth up some other way, the same is

a thief and a robber...I am the door: by me if any man enter in, he shall be saved, and shall go in and out, and find pasture."
- JOHN 10:1-9

Jesus went on to say no one can come to Him unless the Spirit draws them. The Spirit only draws those who are chosen by God. This shows me we did not choose God but God has chosen us.

"According as he hath chosen us in him before the foundation of the world, that we should be holy and without blame before him in love: Having predestinated us unto the adoption of children by Jesus Christ to himself, according to the good pleasure of his will."
- EPHESIANS 1:4-5

Until the Holy Spirit revealed it to me, I didn't understand why God had the children of Israel under the law. The Holy Spirit revealed to me it was because God was their schoolmaster! He had to teach them because most of them only had five-sense knowledge. This is why they wandered around the wilderness for forty years! Only those like Moses and the prophets had a spiritual revelation of God. The Israelites didn't have an intercessor with the Father to help them or the Holy Spirit to guide them. Therefore, God had to give them laws to follow so they would take the correct path.

Since Jesus died, rose again, and now sits on the right hand of the Father, He acts as our intercessor and our attorney. In fact, when satan tries to accuse us before the Father like he did Job, Jesus is our Attorney General and stands up for us and disputes satan's claims. No one is allowed to judge us or accuse us before the Father without

Jesus pleading our case. He was the person of Truth when He walked on earth and Jesus is still the person of Truth today. Jesus can hold this position because He is the only One worthy of that position. The Holy Spirit abiding in us will always be a witness to that fact.

"And I will pray the Father and he shall give you another Comforter, that he may abide with you forever."

- **JOHN 14:16**

That tells me I am never alone because I live in His presence. The Comforter He sends is His Holy Spirit and He is always with me. My going out and my coming in is in Him.

When we don't understand the Word and don't have the knowledge to rightly divide it, we either have not been filled with the Spirit or else we are rebelling against the Spirit. We can rebel against it by refusing to listen when He tries to lead us and by failing to do the things we are commanded to do. We need the knowledge that can only be imparted through the Holy Spirit. So we need to pay close attention to His leading.

"And when he is come, he will reprove the world of sin, and of righteousness, and of judgment: Of sin, because they believe not on me. Of righteousness, because I go to my Father, and ye see me no more; Of judgment, because the prince of this world is judged. I have yet many things to say unto you, but ye cannot bear them now. Howbeit when he, the Spirit of truth, is come, he will guide you into all truth: for he shall not speak of himself; but whatsoever he shall hear, that he shall speak: and he will shew you things to come."

- **JOHN 16:8-13**

Some people think being filled with the Holy Spirit is just to have the ability to speak in tongues. Now, I believe in speaking in tongues as well as the other gifts of the Spirit. I have them operating in my own life. But speaking in tongues is only one of the manifested gifts of the Spirit. I believe it is the everyday leading of the Spirit of truth that is the real evidence of the infilling of the Holy Spirit and it is on this infilling that I depend. I believe in every crisis I face and every battle I fight, the Holy Spirit is there with me leading me into victory and truth. People who don't have this understanding are always calling on Jesus to do this or that for them. If they would just stop and wait upon the Holy Spirit, He would be their Comforter when the storm is raging all about them. He would help them to do for themselves what they have the authority to do through the holy name of Jesus.

In the righteousness of God you are free of fear and satan is defeated. The Holy Spirit will lead you into the truth that satan was defeated at Calvary and stripped of all his power. When we have this knowledge, we don't need to pay attention to satan. We can live in the Spirit as if he did not even exist. We will find if we yield ourselves to the Holy Spirit and allow Him to lead us, we will live a life free from sin, fear, and condemnation. But we must learn to listen to the Holy Spirit. We need to find a quiet place, hold the Bible close to our heart, and thank God for His goodness and His love.

We need to learn not to talk to the Lord as much as wait upon Him and let Him talk to us. Sometimes it is in the wee hours of the morning after everyone else is asleep before the Lord talks to me. But this has brought much spiritual growth into my life. Sometimes the Holy Spirit will lead me to say "I love you Jesus, for all you have done for me." Then I will just meditate on the Word and my cup will run over with spiritual blessings. Other times I will feel like a spiritual giant and the Spirit will show me things that will soon come to pass or will reveal to me what tomorrow holds for me. Most of all, the Holy Spirit reveals to me Jesus is already in my tomorrows, making a way for me.

Being led by the Holy Spirit is the only way to have peace and joy and victory in every battle of life. We need to remind ourselves every day that our body is the temple of the Holy Spirit and the Father and the Son have come to take up abode in us. We need to let go of our yesterdays, live in the present, and operate in "now" faith. We must all come into a place where we are completely guiltless before God. We must be responsive to the Holy Spirit and open and ready at all times to obey His command. It's not wise to make our plans without consulting the Lord. We need to know His will in everything we do. If we seek His will, the Holy Spirit will have free reign in our lives at all times. He will be able to use us in the Father's kingdom work.

The Holy Spirit gives us the assurance we can let our faith rest in every promise of God. And if we are obedient to His commands, He will use us to bless others. Once I was led by the Spirit to travel 1,500 miles to a man's house. I didn't know why the Spirit was telling me to go there. But I got there just in time. The man's wife had planned to kill herself and her children. If I had arrived five minutes later, it would have happened and they would all have been dead.

Another time I was led by the Spirit to just get in my car and drive. I saw a house in the country and the Spirit compelled me to stop. I got out and knocked on the door. No one came to the door but I heard someone groaning. I went inside and found an old man lying under his kitchen table. He lived alone and had suffered a stroke three days earlier. I prayed for him and led him to the Lord and God raised him up.

I could go on and on about the times I have been led by the Holy Spirit to help others. The Holy Spirit has become a companion in the spirit realm of my life. He is my Comforter just as He is the Comforter to all who trust in Jesus. I believe Jesus is coming soon. Until that day, let us all be led by the Holy Spirit and work in the Father's kingdom bringing in the harvest.

God wants you to have His best while on earth and He wants us to give Him our best. If you are not already filled with the Holy Spirit, my prayer is that you will seek to be filled and allow the Holy Spirit to reveal all God has for you. You will find when you are filled with the Spirit, you will never be the same again. You will be able to accomplish goals you were never able to come close to doing before.

14

FELLOWSHIPPING THE HOLY SPIRIT

————

When you become born-again, the old man Adam is dead and you are recreated in the nature of Christ Jesus and in the wisdom of God the Father. You become the "new creation" as spoken of in the New Testament. Before He fashioned creation, it was God's desire to make man in His image and likeness so He could fellowship with Him. I believe this fellowship is one reason for the infilling of the Holy Spirit. God is a Spirit and those fellowshipping with Him must do so in and through the Holy Spirit.

"But the hour cometh, and now is, when the true worshippers shall worship the Father in spirit and in truth: for the Father seeketh such to worship him. God is a Spirit: and they that worship him must worship him in spirit and in truth."

- JOHN 4:23-24

"He came unto his own, and his own received him not. But as many as received him, to them he gave power to become the sons of God, even to them that believe on his name."

- JOHN 1:11-12

You see, as sons of God, we must take on the nature, righteousness, and wisdom of God. He knew we would need a guide so He sent us the Holy Spirit to teach us from the time we are spiritual babes until we come into the full knowledge of His Son Christ Jesus. He will teach us the will of the Father until we know it as fully as Jesus did. Then, through obedience, we will be led by the Spirit of truth and the wisdom of God will give us understanding of the Word that we might have faith to obey it and see God's power in demonstration. The Spirit teaches us if we will be faithful to the Lord's command, we will grow in the righteousness and holiness of God and we will be filled with God's wisdom. Then we will do the works Jesus did and will truly become the "sons of God."

One day while I was praying, it seemed I could not get the breakthrough I needed. But I kept praying and suddenly the Holy Spirit filled the room and I began to pray in the spirit. I didn't understand what I was praying but the answer came just the same. This experience reinforced my understanding that when we are unable to pray, the Holy Spirit intercedes for us.

Another time in my life, when the church needed to borrow some money for the land where our radio station is presently located, every bank in the city turned us down. I didn't know what to do. So on this particular day I was standing in front of the station looking up toward heaven and I said, "Father, what do I do?" Suddenly, like lightning in my spirit, I heard the Father speaking to me; telling me to go to a certain man and explain what I needed. I obeyed the Holy Spirit and the man gave us the money without asking a single question. If I had listened to my five senses instead of the Holy Spirit, I would have said this purchase must not be God's will. But I knew God had told me to buy this land and I have faith that when He speaks, His words are always fulfilled.

So many children of God are living in spiritual poverty because they have been taught the Holy Spirit is not for us today. These people are trying to serve God with their five senses. If five-sense knowledge didn't work in the days of the Israelites, it sure won't work for us today. We need the guidance of the Holy Spirit to survive and live victoriously today just as much as they did in the days when Jesus lived and died.

The Holy Spirit wasn't given just to guide us in the big endeavors of life; but also to guide us in the everyday things. Whether great or small, everything the Spirit does in our life will give glory to Jesus our Lord. Many times the Spirit may show us the Father's will in a vision or a dream. The working of the Holy Spirit in our life will bring God's blessing to us and will also cause others to be blessed through us. Never again will we have to be in bondage to satan or live a life of sin, guilt, or fear because where the Spirit of the Lord is, there is liberty and freedom.

The Holy Spirit teaches us to love and not hate and to give and not take. He does this because this is the very nature of our Father. I believe it pleases Him when His children honor Him by keeping His commandments. And I also believe it pleases Him when His children praise and worship Him in unity. The Father desires for His children to dwell together in unity and worship Him in spirit and truth.

GUIDE ME, HOLY SPIRIT

"...the Father seeketh such to worship Him."

It is reasonable to believe our Father expects His children to come together in praise and worship since He inhabits the praises of His people. The Spirit teaches us the proper way to praise and worship the Father through Jesus Christ our Lord. I believe when Christians depart from true worship in the spirit and begin to worship through sense knowledge, it grieves the heart of the Father. If we do this, we turn into an instrument for the flesh to receive praise. Instead of praising God, people praise the song leader or the musicians and in doing so, move into a carnal or soulish type of worship. But if we are led by the Spirit, this won't happen.

As His children, God wants us to take the time to worship Him and do His will. It is always a mistake to be in a rush when you come to worship the Lord. Patience is necessary in order to receive from the Lord. We should always make sure we have plenty of time to worship our Lord and Sovereign and to listen to what He is teaching us through the Holy Spirit.

Before Adam fell into disobedience in the Garden of Eden, he met with God in the cool of the day for fellowship. I believe our heavenly Father still longs for that kind of fellowship with His children. Sometimes, early in the morning, He will meet with me. Sometimes He meets with me in the evening. In all of my fellowship meetings with ministers, family or friends, none are like the meetings with my heavenly Father. Words cannot express the joy I feel when fellowshipping with Him. Every time we meet, whether in my prayer room or elsewhere, God always blesses me before I leave. Jacob wrestled with an angel of the Lord and would not let him go until he blessed him. But I don't have to wrestle with angels to receive a blessing from my Father. I just have to take the time to meet with Him.

Adam didn't meet with the Lord to present a need because he didn't have any needs. He met with the Lord just to fellowship with Him. It's okay to go to our Father with our needs but we also need to go to Him just to fellowship with Him. When we understand the love of our heavenly Father, we can truthfully say the Lord is our shepherd and we shall not want. Our every need will be met in Him.

There are three stages in spiritual life. They are worship, waiting, and work. We should never jump from one to the other but we should study the life of Jesus and let the Holy Spirit flow through us as we worship the Father. We need to learn to wait on the Lord until He shows us just what it is He has for us to do. Then we should work at it with all our might. I have found it is a great pleasure to obey God when He speaks. By faith, I act upon what He says and the enemy is defeated. I can see great victory just by being obedient and knowing I am pleasing my Father. The Holy Spirit will lead us from victory to victory by the wisdom of God. He will show us the glory of the Father when we have a testimony that pleases Him.

The Holy Spirit will teach us the only place to find rest and true joy is in doing God's will. We will not find any enjoyment in the world's pleasures and activities. The Holy Spirit will never lead us into temptation but will lead us through it as if it did not even exist. He will teach us to resist temptation the same way Jesus did. God the Father cannot be tempted and those who have been led by the Spirit and who understand the righteousness and holiness of God will never be overwhelmed by temptation either. They will live as if satan doesn't exist. Instead, the Holy Spirit will show these individuals the glory of the Father.

The Holy Spirit will remind us we are in this world but we are not of this world. When the Holy Spirit teaches us all Jesus did at Calvary, satan loses his power over us. In the Spirit we have all the authority Jesus had through His name, so we are no longer defeated.

15

THE VICTORIOUS HOLY SPIRIT

God's love makes a difference in the life of every born-again person. God's love gives the believer the power to stand and see His salvation. He gives us protective armor to shield us from the "fiery darts" of the devil.

"Put on the whole armor of God, that ye may be able to stand against the wiles of the devil...having your loins girt about with truth, and having on the breastplate of righteousness; And your feet shod with the preparation of the gospel of peace; Above all, taking the shield of faith, wherewith ye shall be able to quench the fiery darts of the wicked. And take the helmet of salvation and the sword of the Spirit which is the Word of God."
- EPHESIANS 6:11-17

With this armor protecting our spirit man, we need not fear satan or his demons. But we do need to put on this armor of God and wear it at all times as part of God's protection for us. We can't expect protection if we aren't obedient.

We also need to "walk with God" as Enoch did if we are to have His holiness, righteousness and wisdom. This way we will have a testimony that will please God. I don't believe anything extemporaneous took Enoch's eyes off God.

Then look at the prophets Elisha and Elijah. Elijah told Elisha if he saw him when he was taken up that he could have his request of a double portion of the anointing on Elijah. And Elisha did receive a double portion! I want this same double portion, but I know in order to receive it, I must keep "looking unto Jesus the author and finisher of our faith" through the Holy Spirit, to guide me in my journey through life (**HEBREWS 12:1-3**). It is only right that as joint heirs with Christ, we look to Him through the Holy Spirit to lead us into all righteousness.

The Holy Spirit leads us to do the Father's will and to be victorious in every battle. He will teach us how to be totally "sold out" to God so we can walk with Him like Enoch did. Then none of the pleasures of this world will mean anything to us. We will find the only way to obtain real pleasure will be in doing God's will and being led by the Spirit. Then, the power of the Holy Spirit will keep us in the center of God's will.

When we know the person of truth - Jesus, He becomes our righteousness, our holiness, and our wisdom. He also becomes our Healer. If the Healer lives in us and we are totally yielded to the Holy Spirit, then we can walk in health and victory all the days of our life. We can be free from sickness and disease. I learned this late in life after going through many storms and sicknesses. After coming close to death and being told I would not live through the night, I began to understand it is not God's will for me or any of His children to suffer sickness, disease, or satanic opposition.

That night the Holy Spirit unveiled to me the wisdom of Christ in His righteousness and holiness and gave me an understanding of the Father's will. Afterwards, I was inspired to write this book through which I pray God's children will be blessed and live a life of victory abiding in the truth.

Even though Jesus Christ is the Healer, He doesn't actively heal us today. He did that at Calvary almost two thousand years ago, just as He saved us. As we believe in the finished work of Calvary, God confirms His Word and saves and heals us according to our faith. The healing is already there, waiting for us to receive. We don't have to beg for it. All He accomplished at Calvary is ours. Now we need to reach out by faith and take hold of those resources. He is not going to do any more for us than He has already done. Every promise of God is ours when we act on God's Word by faith. God will confirm His Word and bring it to pass in our life. After the Holy Spirit guided me into this truth, He also taught me how to accept that truth and live in freedom from all the powers of the devil. Today the Holy Spirit is using me to teach others how to release their faith in the promises of God and have life more abundantly. This way, the Father will be glorified in the Son. The Father sees His Word being fulfilled in the finished work of Calvary and it must bring much joy to His heart to see His children believing and trusting His Word.

Faith in God brings victory in every battle we face because the Spirit of truth teaches us we are the sons of God if we are led by the Spirit. My heart seeks to know the perfect will of God every day of my life. I seek to please Him as I fellowship with the Father in the Holy Spirit. In Him I find the strength to fight every battle of life and in Him I find rest and peace for my soul. The Holy Spirit teaches us not only how to love and have fellowship with the Father but also how to love and have fellowship with all God's family. He teaches us while we are studying and meditating on God's Word.

When we know this truth it relieves us from worry of any kind. It brings comfort to our spirit to know the Father watches over us and that He loves us with an eternal, never-dying love. When this truth was enlightened to me, I realized knowing this not only sets us free but it would keep us free from sickness, disease, sin, guilt, and all condemnation.

The Holy Spirit will teach us how to apply God's Word in our life as husbands and wives and as mothers and fathers. He will teach men to be the priest of their home and family. Most of all, He will teach men how to love their wives as Christ loved the church and how not to provoke their children to wrath. The Holy Spirit will teach us to bless our family in the same way our heavenly Father blesses us. Men are responsible for not only meeting their families' needs spiritually and physically, but also for protecting them from the powers of satan. I lay my hands on my wife and bless her and I do the same for my children. Every husband and father should do the same thing. When we do this, the Father is pleased and He keeps our family under that blessing.

What a joy it is to know the Father is pleased with us as we seek His heart like David, who was a man after God's own heart (**ACTS 13:14b**). In the heart of God we find shelter from the storm, peace for the mind, and rest for the soul. We will find fellowship with God because He wants us to have fellowship with Him according to His Word. This is the foundation we stand on to meet with Him.

The Holy Spirit will guide us from one revelation to another. But He will always first give us the revelation Peter got from the Father. This revelation is that Jesus is the Christ, the Son of the living God. This is the number one revelation for all born-again Christians and one we should cling to.

"When Jesus came into the coasts of Caesarea Philippi, he asked his disciples, saying, Whom do men say that I the Son of man am? And they said, Some say that thou art John the Baptist: some, Elias; and others, Jeremias, or one of the prophets. He saith unto them, But whom say ye that I am? And Simon Peter answered and said, Thou art the Christ, the Son of the living God. And Jesus answered and said unto him, Blessed art thou, Simon Barjona: for flesh and blood hath not revealed it unto thee, but my Father which is in heaven. And I say also unto thee, That thou art Peter, and upon this rock will I build my church; and the gates of hell will not prevail against it. And I will give unto thee the keys of the kingdom of heaven: and whatsoever thou shalt bind on earth shall be bound in heaven: and whatsoever thou shalt loose on earth shall be loosed in heaven."

- **MATTHEW 16:13-19**

103

What is the foundation on which Jesus told Peter He would build His church? It wasn't Peter who was "the Rock." The foundation of His Church was and is the revelation that Jesus is the Son of the living God. How do we know this is true? The Holy Spirit revealed it to Peter and he in turn explained it in his writings.

"Ye also, as lively stones, are built up a spiritual house, an holy priesthood, to offer up spiritual sacrifices, acceptable to God by Jesus Christ. Wherefore also it is contained in the scripture, Behold, I lay in Zion a chief cornerstone, elect, precious: and he that believeth on him shall not be confounded. Unto you therefore which believe he is precious: but unto them which be disobedient, the stone which the builders disallowed, the same is made the head of the corner."

- **1 PETER 2:5-7**

If any revelation comes before you get this truth, there will be something wrong because to be saved you must believe Jesus is the Christ, the Son of God. Notice Jesus' words regarding the way to salvation.

"Verily, verily, I say unto you, He that entereth not by the door into the sheepfold, but climbeth up some other way, the same is a thief and a robber."

- **JOHN 10:1**

This truth opens your heart for the Holy Spirit to reveal Christ's wisdom, righteousness, and holiness. As you yield to the leadership of the Holy Spirit, you will have a clear understanding of God's will and plan for your life. Truly yielding to the Holy Spirit allows Him to guide you according to God's perfect plan for your life.

16

THE CHALLENGE OF THE HOLY SPIRIT

———

The Holy Spirit is many things and He plays a most important part in every born-again Christian's life. Not only is He a guide but also a revealer. He will take what is in the mind and heart of God and reveal it to us. The Holy Spirit is a power-giver because He gives us the power to become the sons of God.

"But as many as received him, to them gave he power to become the sons of God, even to them that believe on his name."
                                                                - JOHN 1:12

Can you imagine what it means to become the sons of God? It means we will have knowledge of the truth which will bring power to the soul of every believer. We will have a knowledge which will bring us out of the darkness and into the light (**1 PETER 2:9**). Where we have been void of understanding, now we will know the truth about God's will for each of us and that will set us free to worship in spirit and truth.

When we take on the nature of God, we will have no desire for the things of this world. We will be spiritually-oriented and spiritually-discerning. We will be able to truly fellowship with the Father just as Adam and Eve did prior to the fall in the Garden in Eden. In that realm, we will enjoy true peace and contentment in the Lord. On the other hand, the natural man can only receive knowledge through his five senses. He doesn't receive spiritual knowledge because he cannot accept anything he cannot see, smell, hear, taste, or feel.

We should never run ahead of God's guidance. If there is the slightest possibility it is not the Holy Spirit guiding us, we need to stop and stand still. My dad gave me some excellent advice when I first started preaching the gospel. He said, "Son, don't get ahead of God but always be led of His Spirit." I have always tried to do this. There have been times I had to break fellowship with people because they didn't understand what I was doing. Many times I had to say "no" to those who tried to tell me how and what to preach and what to do to make my ministry bigger and better. But I have learned to be led only by the Holy Spirit. I know if I would be willing to compromise the truth, I could have a ministry making millions of dollars. The devil has already made me that offer. But I would have to quit baptizing in Jesus' name and steer away from holiness and I won't do that! I won't compromise the truth for profit any more than Jesus would. I won't say "thus saith the Lord" if God doesn't say it. If I did, it would be a lie and I would be no better than satan, who is the father of lies. I will continue to teach holiness because it's a requirement of every born-again Christian. Now I'm not talking about fanatical or outward holiness, but rather genuine holiness which emphasizes the inner spirit of man.

If we get holy on the inside first, I guarantee we will be dressed holy and decent on the outside. All we need to know is how to serve God, how to be led by the Spirit, how not to quench or grieve the Spirit, and how to come together in one accord. Sometimes this last one, (coming together in one accord) is the hardest to do.

There may be times you have to change your job or do other things in order to do God's will. But whatever you have to do, if you are obedient to God, it will pay off in the end. If you trust in the natural man's sense knowledge, you will deny Jesus somewhere along the way just as Peter did. We read how Jesus warned His followers of what was to come. He knew they loved Him but He knew their human nature was weak and they would need help to stand.

"Then saith Jesus unto them, All ye shall be offended because of me this night: because it is written, I will smite the shepherd, and the sheep of the flock shall be scattered abroad. But after I am risen again, I will go before you into Galilee. Peter answered and said unto him, Though all men shall be offended because of thee, yet will I never be offended. Jesus said unto him, Verily, I say unto thee, That this night, before the cock crow, thou shalt deny me thrice. Peter said unto him, Though I should die with thee, yet will I not deny thee..."
- MATTHEW 26:31-35

Peter loved Jesus with all his heart but he did not know what his flesh was capable of doing. He told Jesus he would never forsake him and yet, at the time when he became frightened, he was unable to stand strong for Jesus. Afterwards, he was crushed at his inability to stand (**MATTHEW 26:75**). This doesn't mean Peter was not a faithful Apostle or that he wasn't truly surrendered to Jesus.

It was because he didn't have the Holy Spirit at that time. He only relied on sense knowledge and not the power of the Holy Spirit. We can do nothing under our own power but only in the name and power of Jesus. If all we have is sense knowledge, we have no power because sense knowledge is void of power. We cannot stand without the Holy Spirit.

When Jesus gives you something to do, don't try to accomplish it in yourself. If you do, you will fail miserably. Instead, keep your eyes forward on the Lord Jesus Christ and know it is only through His power that we can finish the task He has given us to do. Wait upon the Lord and He will renew your strength. The Holy Spirit will always bring to our remembrance the words of Christ. He will never add to those words or take away from them. He was given to us so the Word of God could be fulfilled in our life.

In my forty years of ministry, I have seen ministers preach under the anointing of God and, when the anointing would lift, would try to keep going. This is wrong! When the anointing lifts, the Spirit is saying the people have had enough for this time and God has blessed all He is going to bless that day. We can't force the anointing any more than we can do God's work successfully without it. We have to remember Jesus was totally led by the Spirit and He was our example. If we are totally guided by the Spirit, we will please the Father because the only way to please Him is to walk in the light of His Word.

17

THE VOICE
OF THE HOLY SPIRIT

———

Many years ago, I was having a crusade in Canada. Dr. Alexander Ness came to the airport to pick me up and take me to the church. I had been praying about something bothersome I had seen going on in the ministry of divine healing and I had not had a breakthrough. I was just sitting there thinking about this certain evangelist and I looked over at Dr. Ness and said "How do you like this evangelist?" In that characteristic, solemn voice of his, Dr. Ness replied, "When I was filled with the Holy Spirit, I lost my likes and dislikes." He didn't say another word and neither did I. With that one statement he was saying that when he started being led by the Spirit of God, he didn't have time to judge others. That was a prime example of being led by the Spirit.

When John came to Jesus and said he saw someone casting out devils; he told Jesus they had forbidden this perceived outsider to continue. But Jesus told the disciples to leave him alone.

"...for he that is not against us is for us."

- **LUKE 9:50b**

If we are led by the Spirit, we will have the same attitude toward others. We will be kept busy by the Holy Spirit, doing the Father's will and taking care of things pertaining to the kingdom of God. We won't have time to judge others. We will never find enmity and strife in the Holy Spirit but we will always find the fruits of the Spirit, including righteousness, peace, and joy.

We will find when the Holy Spirit leads us to do something, it is always for God's glory and not man's adulation. The Holy Spirit will never bring praise to the person even if people try to lift up an individual instead of Christ. If we are born-again believers, we will never accept any honor and praise because we know it will grieve the Holy Spirit. Being a born-again believer will humble us because we have been taught by the Spirit that taking honor and glory from God is not right (**ISAIAH 48:11**).

The Holy Spirit is the Spirit of truth. He came to teach man to love, to care, and to rule over all the powers of satan including sickness, fear, and failure. He came to teach us to be victorious in every battle we face. He came so we might have springs of living water flowing from our innermost being. When we walk by faith, we have no fear of anything or anyone because we know "greater is he that is in you than he that is in the world."

Some preachers constantly remind people to be careful not to sin or fall into the lust of the flesh. I don't do this because I don't believe Jesus had to worry about falling into such things even though he lived as a man. I believe He was a one hundred percent man of faith. He was made flesh, lived in the world, and was tempted in the same manner as we are but He didn't go about wondering if satan would win the next battle. And neither should a person led by the Spirit worry about these things. However, we should never neglect the importance of our prayer life. It's the most important part of our day. The disciples asked Jesus if He would teach them how to pray. Jesus taught them to pray after this manner:

"Our Father, which is in heaven, hallowed be thy name. Thy kingdom come, thy will be done, on earth as it is in heaven. Give us this day our daily bread. Forgive us our debts as we forgive our debtors. And lead us not into temptation but deliver us from evil: for thine is the kingdom and the power and the glory forever. Amen."

- **MATTHEW 6:9-13**

Although the Word says man ought to pray without ceasing, we need to make it short, get our mind on the Spirit, and go into the battle a winner. Don't go into any battle if there is the least bit of doubt God is leading you. If someone comes to you and says, "I have a word from the Lord", the Spirit of truth in you will bear witness if it is a true "word." Always listen to the Holy Spirit and you will never go wrong.

The Holy Spirit will never start you across a valley and leave you to navigate it alone. He will never lead you to the mountain and say, "This is it. Climb it." Neither will He leave you to face the storm alone. God doesn't make His obedient children sick. He keeps them from getting sick. I believe Jesus is in your storm to calm it, not to watch you struggle. He passes by your bed to make it in the time of your affliction, not to watch you lay there. He wants us to be more than conquerors through Christ Jesus who strengthens us. If we are sitting in heavenly places with

Him, we are living in the righteousness of God, having the very nature of Christ and having God-given power over all the powers of darkness.

If the same Spirit that raised Jesus from the dead dwells within us, it will quicken our mortal bodies. The resurrection power lives within us, but if the devil can convince us it was not a completely finished work at Calvary, then he can steal our power and cause us to fall at his command. However, as long as we abide in God's love, we will never be conquered by satan. Continually remind yourself - Jesus defeated satan once and for all time at Calvary. As long as we are inside God's righteousness and His holiness, we can stand against the devil and he cannot touch us. But if we get outside God's righteousness and holiness, we cannot stand against the forces of darkness. It is only when you have the Holy Spirit within you and the faith of the Son of God, that you can walk in victory and live every day as a winner. When our life is dominated by God, we will speak as the Spirit gives utterance and our ability will be unlimited. We will have victory in all things at all times. We can have a testimony like Jesus did to Nicodemus,

"We speak that which we do know, and testify that we have seen..."
                                                              - JOHN 3:11

Enoch did not have to fight with the devil in order to walk with God. He walked with God by faith as if satan didn't even exist. We need to do this today. What a waste of time when we try to win a battle that has already been fought and won by the King of Kings and Lord of Lords!

Jesus' love for the Father caused Him to do the Father's will even to the point of dying on the cross. This demonstrates to us that the fullness of the Godhead dwells bodily in Christ. He has the wisdom of God, the nature of God, and the love of God. The nature of God is love and to love the Father is wisdom.

Anyone who has not reached their place in the righteousness and holiness of God, will try to serve God through sense knowledge. They won't be walking in the Spirit and therefore cannot attain victory in all things. The prodigal son would have never left home and wasted his inheritance had he not been living and operating in the realm of his five-sense knowledge. But as the Holy Spirit teaches and guides us into all truth, we learn to listen to the inner man and begin to live by faith and not by sight and sense knowledge. When Jesus said He would send another Comforter, He was telling His followers to follow His leadership and be led by the Holy Spirit. He wanted them to listen to the Spirit. Likewise, He wants us to be ready at all times to listen to the Spirit and act on the Word of God by faith.

Enoch Nelson became a missionary late in life. He taught at our School of Ministry and told how he started over four hundred churches in one year. One day I asked him to what he attributed this accomplishment and he answered without hesitation, "When God, the Holy Spirit speaks, I act." This is the right idea. When the Lord speaks to you, don't pray about it, just act on His word! God's Word does not need praying over! It is already settled forever in heaven and should be settled in the heart of every born-again believer. Someone once asked me how I know it is the Lord speaking to me and not the devil. That answer can be found directly from scripture.

"And when he brings out his own sheep, he goes before them; and the sheep follow him, for they know his voice. Yet they will by no means follow a stranger, but will flee from him for they do not know the voice of strangers. I am the good shepherd; and I know My sheep, and am known by My own."
- JOHN 10:4-5,14

I am one of His sheep and I know His voice. I know my inner man won't respond to any other voice in the spirit world. But be careful what voices you listen to while in the realm of the five senses. The voices you hear through sense knowledge could very well be the voice of darkness operating as the angel of light.

The Holy Spirit taught me a valuable lesson about listening to God and doing His will. As a young man, I was a building contractor in Atlanta, Georgia. I had been running from the call of God in my life for a long time. I was waiting for a more convenient time to serve God and expected God to let me go on running like this without consequence. But God had other plans. I've often heard God gets your attention in dramatic ways and He certainly got my attention on the way to work one day. I had stopped at a crossroads and suddenly just fell over in the seat of my truck.

The next thing I knew, I was in the hospital listening to the doctor tell me I had less than six months to live. That certainly got my attention and it took all the wind out of my sails. I cried out to God but no answer came. It seemed the heavens were brass. I kept on crying out to

God and repenting for my wrongs and finally the Lord spoke to me. He said, "You have made three vows to me and you have broken each one of them." I begged God to give me another chance and He did. I learned my lesson that day and I never again made a vow to God that I broke. The Word tells us it is better not to make a vow than to make one and break it (**ECCLESIASTES 5:2-7**). The Lord was merciful to me. He healed me and I immediately began making plans to go into the full-time ministry.

After going out of business, my wife and I had $200.00 left to live on and the Lord was leading us to go minister in Florida. We were getting ready to leave but the devil wasn't finished. The night before we left, temptation came knocking on our door. I got a call from a builder friend. He said, "If you will promise not to go into the ministry, I will make out a will and leave everything I own to you at my death. I am already worth $750,000 and it will all be yours if you will just stay and work with me." He went on to offer me a good salary, a new truck, and a house with four bedrooms and three baths.

Now, you have to understand, this was a big deal back then. I was raised in the country with an outhouse instead of an inside bathroom. We took baths in a #10 washtub or else in the river on Sunday because we didn't have indoor plumbing. But I couldn't even entertain the thought of accepting this offer. The Holy Spirit had taught me a more valuable lesson and I had learned it well. I had made a vow to God and I intended to keep it.

The Holy Spirit had prepared me by letting me know when a Christian says "yes" to the call of God, satan shows up and begins to work on the five senses. He shows you a world of success and makes you an offer he thinks you can't refuse, like he did after Jesus had fasted for forty days. But just as Jesus overcame the devil by telling him what the Word said, we can do the same thing. That's the reason we need to read the Bible and meditate on it every day. We need to have the same attitude David had when he said,

"Thy Word have I hid in mine heart, that I might not sin against thee."

- PSALM 119:11

If you hide the Word of God in your heart, satan can't steal it from you. Your faith will be standing in nothing but God and His Word and He will always lead you to victory.

So being led by the Holy Spirit, my wife and I and Brother Joe Kerbow left for Florida the next morning. The only person we knew in Tampa, Florida was Brother Sam Fuller. We drove to his home and when we arrived, he was getting in his truck to leave. We told him what we were doing and he said, "That's strange because I was just going down to the utility department to have the lights and water turned off in my mother's house. She left this morning to go back to Georgia for awhile." We moved into his mother's house and worked for Brother Fuller for a short while, waiting on the Spirit to show us what to do.

I learned Brother Jenkins, another Brother from the Atlanta area that I knew very well, was having a tent meeting in Tampa at the time. We joined his team and after about three months the Holy Spirit spoke and said it was time for us to leave Tampa. Brother Jenkins moved his tent to Bradenton, Florida and just as we finished packing the car to leave, Brother Fuller's mother drove up. Now, she didn't even know we had been living in her house! She just felt it was time for her to return home. God's timing is always just right!

We arrived in Bradenton without a place to stay but the Holy Spirit led us to a Church of God Sister who had a vacant apartment. She told us she had three people who had wanted to rent the apartment but every time she started to rent it the Holy Spirit would say, "No, I have other plans." She gave us the apartment rent-free and we moved in right away. God always provides for His people if we obey Him. When you are led by the Spirit, you will always have peace and rest. It won't matter if the storm is raging around you or if you are in the heat of the battle. You will have the assurance that victory lies just ahead. Many people are always just one step away from their miracle because they are moving in five-sense knowledge instead of being led by the Spirit.

A good example of operating in the five senses is found in the life of the Apostle Peter. He asked Jesus if he could come to Him on the water and Jesus bid him come. Peter began to walk on the surface of the water but when he realized what he was doing, his five senses told him it was impossible and he began to sink under the waves. Peter had stopped operating in faith and had begun to operate in five-sense knowledge! As soon as Peter cried out, the Lord took him by the hand and led him back aboard the ship. Peter learned when you operate in five-sense knowledge, you need Jesus to hold your hand constantly. The same is true for us. When we act in faith on God's Word, we will be able to do the things Jesus did and even greater things because He told His disciples this would happen after He returned to the Father.

We must surrender to the Father's perfect will and be led by the Holy Spirit. Jesus was our example and we need to follow in His footsteps and do the Father's will. We won't have any problem doing this if we take on the nature of God and abide in His agapé love. It is a wonderful feeling to know your heavenly Father is pleased with you. What a joy it brings to the heart to know we not only fellowship with Him but have a relationship with Him as His sons and daughters. When our faith is made perfect (or complete) we will have one hundred percent faith in God's Word and never have a problem obeying it or acting upon it in any crisis we face. Jesus passed the test for all of us when He defeated satan at Calvary. If we accept Him as our substitute and believe He paid the price for us all, we are not losers but winners in His name.

We need the Holy Spirit to perfect our faith. There may be whole tracts of stubbornness and ignorance in each one of us that must be revealed by the Holy Spirit. These can only be revealed when Jesus gets us alone. Sometimes it takes things happening in our lives before it can take place. Does God need to get your attention? It might be losing a job or becoming sick or even getting to a place where you don't know what to do or which way to turn in your life.

There was a time in my life when I was so busy working for the Lord, I didn't have time to get alone with Him. I came down with heart problems and was given up to die. While I was sick in bed, I got alone with Jesus and read the Bible through in seven weeks. During this time of rest, God changed the entire focus of my ministry and life.

Now, I'm never too busy to stop and spend time alone with my Lord. I love to be alone with my Father. I love every minute in His presence and love being taught by Him. The Holy Spirit will be with you in every battle you face and will see to it that you are a winner. But you need to spend time alone with Jesus to know what He wants you to do.

18

GUIDE ME, HOLY SPIRIT

———

How can you know the divine guidance of the Holy Spirit in your everyday life? While God's purpose for each individual may differ, there are some practical ways to discern the operation of the Holy Spirit.

PRAY TO BE LED BY THE HOLY SPIRIT

It is only in surrendering to His will that you allow yourself to be under the divine control of the Holy Spirit. I've often referred to the Holy Spirit as a "gentleman." He will not go where He is not invited. He will not supercede your will. He operates in strict accordance to the Word of God. He moves in the agapé love of God. You must give Him the reins of your life if you desire His leadership and guidance. Look at how Jesus instructed His disciples to pray.

"And lead us not into temptation, but deliver us from evil..."
- MATTHEW 6:13

By daily surrendering your will to God and giving the Holy Spirit permission to chart the course of your day, you open up exciting possibilities for the supernatural to take place. Praying this prayer also keeps you in divine protection.

"Order my steps in thy word: and let not any iniquity have dominion over me."
— **PSALM 119:133**

"The steps of a good man are ordered by the LORD: and he delighteth in his way. Though he fall, he shall not be utterly cast down: for the LORD upholdeth him with his hand."
— **PSALM 37:23-24**

You can be assured the Holy Spirit knows how to guide and keep you in the will of God if you are submitted to Him!

THE HOLY SPIRIT WILL NEVER GUIDE YOU CONTRARY TO SCRIPTURE

The Bible is the revealing of God to us. It is the divinely inspired roadmap of life. It details God's will to the believer. The Holy Spirit's guidance will always "mirror" the Word of God. Begin by doing those things the Bible instructs and watch the Spirit open up the window of revelation in your life.

"And hereby we do know that we know him, if we keep his commandments. He that saith, I know him, and keepeth not his commandments, is a liar, and the truth is not in him. But

whoso keepeth his word, in him verily is the love of God perfected: hereby know we that we are in him."
- **1 JOHN 2:3-5**

Because the Holy Spirit is in complete unity with God, His leadership in your life is based on the Word. Any spirit that tries to lead you contrary to that Word is a deceiving spirit. Check or "try the spirits" as instructed in **1 JOHN 4:1-3**. The Holy Spirit will always be in 100% agreement with the Word of God.

TRUST IN THE HOLY SPIRIT'S GUIDANCE

There will be times when the Spirit is leading in direct opposition to what your five senses are telling you. It is in those times you must be totally resigned to follow His guidance and not your own understanding.

"Trust in the LORD with all thine heart; and lean not unto thine own understanding. In all thy ways acknowledge him, and he shall direct thy paths. Be not wise in thine own eyes: fear the LORD, and depart from evil. It shall be health to thy navel, and marrow to thy bones."
- **PROVERBS 3:5-8**

In our five senses, we can only mess up what God has planned. Take Abraham for example. The promise of a son which would make him the father of many nations could not be comprehended by this elderly patriarch and his wife Sarah. So they devised a way to bring God's plan to pass. We all know what happened.

When you are sure you have heard the voice of the Holy Spirit, trust that God's ways are much higher than our ways. Our finite minds cannot begin to comprehend the magnitude of His plan and design for our lives. Don't try to figure out God. Have faith beyond your human reasoning for we know that

"...all things work together for good to them that love God, to them who are the called according to his purpose."
- **ROMANS 8:28**

LOOK FOR THE OPPORTUNITIES THE HOLY SPIRIT PRESENTS AND BE READY TO RESPOND TO HIS DIRECTION

"But watch thou in all things...make full proof of thy ministry."
- **2 TIMOTHY 4:5**

The Apostle Paul was trying to make the young disciple Timothy aware of the possibilities for serving God. Just a few verses earlier, he expressed the importance of being "instant in season, out of season." (**VS.2**) Often we miss the Holy Spirit by passing up the small chances He brings up to witness, to do good, to give a kind word, or be a strength to one who is weak. Part of being obedient to the Lord is responding to the still, small voice of His Spirit.

"This is a faithful saying, and these things I will that thou affirm constantly, that they which have believed in God might be careful to maintain good works. These things are good and

profitable unto men."

- TITUS 3:8

Be ready to be responsive to the guidance and direction of the Spirit. Then start looking around. You may be surprised at what you see when you start looking through the eyes of the Holy Spirit and not just your human eyesight.

DETERMINE TO BREAK OUT OF YOUR DAILY "GRIND" FOR MOMENTS OF SPIRITUAL REFLECTION AND MEDITATION

We get so hung up in our routines through habit. And not all habits are necessarily bad. Daniel habitually took time to pray three times each day. We find it was one of the secrets to Daniel's success in an environment of ungodliness and power struggles. This daily reflection allowed Daniel to refocus and maintain a refreshing relationship with the Lord.

"Blessed is the man that walketh not in the counsel of the ungodly, nor standeth in the way of sinners, nor sitteth in the seat of the scornful. But his delight is in the law of the LORD; and in his law doth he meditate day and night. And he shall be like a tree planted by the rivers of water, that bringeth forth his fruit in his season; his leaf also shall not wither; and whatsoever he doeth shall prosper."

- PSALM 1:1-3

*"Meditate upon these things (**VS.12-14**); give thyself wholly to them; that thy profiting may appear to all."*
- 1 TIMOTHY 4:15

I have discovered God speaks when we are still enough to listen. By pausing to reflect quietly on the Lord, the Holy Spirit tunes our spiritual "receiver" to the proper channel where our instruction and guidance is being broadcasted.

GIVE HIM THE PRAISE AND HONOR FOR HIS GUIDANCE

Our human abilities are limited by our physical strengths. But in the Spirit, we have an unlimited resource. You must recognize and honor God for this supernatural ability. Be thankful for His guidance and do it often.

"That ye might walk worthy of the Lord unto all pleasing, being fruitful in every good work, and increasing in the knowledge of God; strengthened with all might, according to his glorious power, unto all patience and longsuffering with joyfulness; Giving thanks unto the Father, which hath made us meet to be partakers of the inheritance of the saints in light."
- COLOSSIANS 1:10-12

Where does our ability and enabling come from? The five senses are not equipped to be "all patient and longsuffering with joyfulness." That only comes through the imparting of God's supernatural power. As a believer, you are a partaker of an inheritance of divine power by the Holy Spirit. Recognize it is Him doing the work in you

126

and not yourself. It will stop pride from developing and keep the Holy Spirit's guidance flowing in your life.

DO EVERYTHING AS UNTO THE LORD

The Apostle Paul described himself as a "prisoner of the Lord (**EPHESIANS 4:1**)." He had come to the full realization of the calling God had placed on his life and wanted nothing else but to fulfill His plan. The Holy Spirit cannot manifest God's purpose and meaning in life when you live for yourself.

"What? Know ye not that your body is the temple of the Holy Ghost which is in you, which ye have of God, and ye are not your own? For ye are bought with a price: therefore glorify God in your body, and in your spirit, which are God's."
                                              - **1 CORINTHIANS 6:19-20**

Live your life as unto God. Let your life exemplify the Holy Spirit's guidance by

"...whatsoever you do in word or deed, do all in the name of the Lord Jesus, giving thanks to God and the Father by him."
                                              - **COLOSSIANS 3:17**

19

CONCLUSION

Under the new covenant which replaced the Law at Jesus death, the Holy Spirit guides us into a great revelation. He teaches us one of the most important things to a believer, and to the heart, is to be ruled by the new kind of love, agapé love. Under this new covenant, the Holy Spirit reveals the three parts of God to us: God for us, God with us, and God in us. This guarantees us God's righteousness, holiness, and wisdom in all areas of our life. It guarantees we will be victorious in everything we set our hands to do. It guarantees we will be the head and not the tail.

If we are the head and not the tail, we will give orders to the devil and not take orders from him. We will be the ones in charge, living the life of an overcomer, and serving God as if the devil didn't even exist. Though satan is still loose today, the only way he can gain power over a born-again Christian is for you to fear him. Remember, there is no fear in perfect love and agapé love is a perfect love. We will be winners because we are the sons of God.

Every believer who is led by the Spirit is a winner because whom the Son has made free is free indeed. We are not to be in bondage in any way in our life. We are free from guilt, sin, sickness, and condemnation because we know Jesus, the personification of truth and righteousness. By abiding in Christ and letting His Word come alive in us, we can ask anything in Jesus' name and it will be done. We will have power over the devil just as Jesus did and we will understand our legal rights as sons of God. The devil tries to leave his influence everywhere he goes. His legion of fallen angels are out there working with him. This is how he makes people believe he is omnipresent. What a liar satan is! God's Word declares he is a liar and the father of lies (**JOHN 8:44b**). Nothing he says can or should be believed. We shouldn't even listen to him. Jesus defeated him and stripped him of his power at Calvary and because of this finished work of deliverance, he is defeated in our lives, too!

Saul was a sincere man who made a mistake when he put Christians to death in Rome. He thought he was doing right but when he met with Christ on the road to Damascus, his mistake was revealed. After he was baptized and filled with the Holy Spirit, Paul had the courage to live with his mistake. He repented and God forgave him and used him in a mighty way. The Apostle Paul allowed himself to be led by the Spirit and was blessed as a result. Likewise, when we come to Christ and He forgives our sins, the only one living with your past is you. God does not live in the past with us and the Holy Spirit will never lead us into the past. He lives only in the present and the future. When God forgives you for those mistakes, He never remembers them or holds them against you. We don't need be afraid that God doesn't know what we've gone through. All those things satan did to hurt you, God knows about it because His guardian angels were there when you suffered the abuse. He forgives and forgets! Each of us, as born-again Christians, should have the courage to live with our mistakes, knowing we have been forgiven. Otherwise, these mistakes will rob us of the blessing of being led of the Lord through His Spirit.

Jesus died to redeem us back to the Father and to the fellowship God had with Adam and Eve in the Garden of Eden. Our Heavenly Father offers us the same relationship He had with Jesus while on earth. Do you remember Jesus' statement in **JOHN 10:10** when He said He came that we "might have life and it more abundantly?" In the Greek text, which is the language this was originally translated from, the word "life" comes from "Zoë" which literally means, "to have the very life of the Father." After His resurrection, Jesus made the declaration,

"All power has been given unto me in heaven and in earth."
- **MATTHEW 28:18**

This was after He took His blood to the mercy seat of God. Jesus was saying His power is in His name. And we have the right to use His name and the power it contains if we are born-again believers and following the leading of the Holy Spirit. Jesus is the Word and we can access the Word as born-again believers. He is in the Holy Spirit and we can use the power of the Holy Spirit just by asking in Jesus' name. These are the three major offices of God. He says He is in His name, His Word, and His Holy Spirit. And He offers us the use of all these in order to be victorious in this life.

When Jesus was instructing His disciples, He said the Holy Spirit would be with us at all times. He also warned the disciples they would face battles. They would be persecuted and taken before the courts. But He told them not to worry about what to say because the Holy Spirit would be present to help them.

"But when they deliver you up, take no thought how or what ye shall speak: for it shall be given you in that same hour what ye shall speak. For it is not ye that speak, but the Spirit of your Father which speaketh in you."

- **MATTHEW 10:19-20**

"If God be for us, who can be against us?"

- **ROMANS 8:31**

I have heard ministers teach that sometimes you can stand and sometimes you just have to fall. I don't believe that. I believe the only time a born-again believer must fall is when they try to stand alone without Jesus. The Word of God says we should take heed lest we fall but it does not say we must fall. When we move away from being led by the Spirit and begin to lean on our own understanding, (trusting in our five-sense knowledge), we are in danger of falling. In that position, we will be like those who stopped following Jesus because their spirit could not receive what Jesus was teaching. Many of the believers and Jews in Capernaum could not accept Jesus was the Son of God. Remember when they left, Jesus asked the twelve disciples,

"Will ye also go away? Then Simon Peter answered him, Lord, to whom shall we go? Thou hast the words of eternal life. And we believe and are sure that thou art that Christ, the Son of the living God."

- **JOHN 6:67b-69**

Peter didn't want to leave the Word and be in danger of falling. In that instance, he stood firm for Jesus because he understood, in the spirit, what Jesus was saying. But the natural man cannot understand these spiritual things. Therefore, the things Jesus taught meant nothing to those who were not born-again. The Holy Spirit will lead you to Christ, reveal Him to you as the Son of the living God, and then help you with this understanding to build a foundation of faith. When we come into the fullness of Christ, having the knowledge of the truth and the blessings of the Son of God, we can worship Him in righteousness, holiness, and wisdom. We come into a true fellowship with God as His sons and daughters.

In order to receive the fullness of Christ it is necessary we be filled with the Holy Spirit and follow His leading. This infilling can take many forms and can affect the person in different ways. But it always leads a person closer to Jesus.

When we become truly hungry for the things of God we will find we have lost our appetite for the things of the world. Then God will speak to us and give us the Holy Spirit to guide us in all truth. The Holy Spirit will teach us about Christ's mission, how He was sent into this world, and will reveal to us God's perfect will for our life.

When we know God's perfect will for us and follow the leading of the Holy Spirit, we will no longer rely on our five-sense knowledge but rather the mind of Christ. Then whatever we do, we cannot be a failure because the Holy Spirit abides in us. We may not always take advantage of all that could be ours but that's not God's fault; it's ours. He wants us to be the head and not the tail. But he won't force us to accept what He has provided for us.

The Holy Spirit spoke to me one day and revealed to me a wonderful truth. He explained what it meant to say, "I am indwelt by God." It means I have God's nature and the very life of the Father. It means I am what He says I am...a temple of the Holy Spirit. And it means I can do all things through Christ who strengthens me. I do not have to have faith for that which already belongs to me. It is mine already because I belong to Jesus. If I belong to Jesus, this means I belong to the Father. Jesus said, "What the Father has is mine and what I have belongs to the Father." This means my very being is God's. My family is His, my children are His, and I am only raising them for His glory. This means He gave us His love, His nature, His righteousness, His holiness, and His blessings.

If we belong to God, then He has prepared a place for us with Him in heaven. We are truly joint heirs with Christ. What a wonderful heritage we have to look forward to. But sometimes I believe we spend so much time talking about heaven and what we are missing out on, that we forget to appreciate what we have here on earth.

"Blessed are the meek: for they shall inherit the earth."
- **MATTHEW 6:5**

We don't have to wait for heaven. We have an inheritance while here on earth. Think about it!

God has always had "supermen" in every period of history. Look at Abraham, Isaac and Jacob, Noah, Elijah and Elisha, and King David. Now I'm not claiming to be a superman or like the prophets of old. But I do have the courage to reach out and take what God makes available for me. That's why the doctors called me "superman" after they told me and my wife I could not possibly live through the night at St. Joseph's Hospital. They told us there was no hope outside of Christ.

During this time I thought about Abraham and Sarah. I remembered how their youth was restored; how Sarah had a child in her old age. I remembered Joshua, Samuel, Daniel, and other men of old who were just ordinary men until there was a job to do. Then they took courage in hand and did the job. All this was going through my mind when the doctors sent me home to die. I knew what they had said but I also knew what God had said. You see, the night I was supposed to die, I had a vision. Written on the wall, I saw these words: **YOUR FAITH**. I heard a small voice say "I am the defender of your faith." I grabbed hold of those words and held on, literally, for my life.

Today, I am a better and healthier man than I was before I got sick. The Holy Spirit has guided me into a place with my heavenly Father where I have never walked before. I am at this current writing, sixty-six years old. And the Spirit is still teaching me about the things of God that make me want to live in His presence and never leave it. I love the Word of God and so should every born-again believer. If we don't love the Word of God and His commandments, we don't love God because He and His Word are one.

The Word of God is the original Seed of God. It is the very essence of God. The Word reveals the mind of the Father to us. The Word of God shows us the way to the Father through Christ Jesus. It is the Father speaking to us; Bread of Life from heaven. The Word of God takes on all we ask the Father to do in Jesus' name and by faith, brings it to pass. The Word of God discerns the inner thoughts of the heart. I don't know what His Word means to anyone else but the following are just a few thoughts of what it means to me.

His Word to me is life eternal.
His Word to me is love.
His Word to me is righteousness.
His Word to me is holiness.
His Word to me is peace.
His Word to me is joy and strength.
His Word to me is power.
His Word to me is victory.
His Word to me is health.
His Word to me is wealth.
His Word to me is family happiness.
His Word to me is a hiding place in the cleft of the rock.
His Word to me is a shelter in the storms.
His Word to me is victory over the devil.
His Word to me means I am a son of God.
His Word to me is heaven.
His Word to me is a mansion in the Father's house.
His Word to me is walking on a street of pure gold.
His Word to me is a river of life.
His Word to me is sitting in heavenly places.
His Word to me is ruling and reigning with Christ.
His Word to me is doing His will.
His Word to me is loving him with all my heart, soul, and mind.
His Word to me is loving my brothers and sisters.
His Word to me is walking with Him as Enoch did.
His Word to me is preaching the gospel.
His Word to me is healing the sick.
His Word to me is casting out devils.

His Word to me is the sure foundation.
His Word to me is the Lord, my Shepherd.
His Word to me is the Son of righteousness with healing in his wings.
His Word to me means I never again have to live a defeated life or be afraid of the devil.
His Word to me is wisdom.
His Word to me is freedom.
His Word to me is everything in life.

The Word of God tells me how Jesus defeated satan at Calvary and stripped him of all his powers. It tells me Jesus holds the keys of death and hell today. The Word of God tells me all I need to know to serve God and live a victorious life in Christ Jesus.

When I was a young Christian, I didn't know the Word of God. I had to depend on what man told me it said. But as time went on, I studied the Word. I meditated upon it. The Holy Spirit began to teach me in-depth about the things of God's Word. Most importantly, He taught me to love the Word of God. I fell in love with it so deeply, I started sleeping with my Bible in my arms each night. I still do this. And when I meditate on the Word, I feel as if Jesus is right there in the room with me.

After I started preaching, I used to sit for hours under the old oak tree in our backyard and listen to dad talk about the Lord and how the Holy Ghost had taught him to trust in the Word of God and how to be led by the Spirit. My dad was not a literate man but the Spirit showed him the Holy Ghost was for our generation and that healing was the children's bread. Often he would say "Son, don't ever doubt God's Word. Trust Him to be your provider in everything."

There were many times my dad would go with me when I was preaching under a tent or in a church. We would always pray for the sick together. Through my dad, the Holy Spirit taught me many things I still hold to and cherish today. My father had faith like no other man I knew growing up. It was such a joy to have him stand by my side and together see the sick healed. He was so filled with the Holy Spirit that it never occurred to him to fear any man or demon.

I remember once when I was holding a revival in the Church of God, a demon-possessed man ran everyone out of the church, including the pastor. Only dad, myself, and a truck driver who had just recently been saved, was left. This demon-possessed man tried to fight my dad but by the power of the Holy Spirit, dad cast the devil out of him. Like the man who had the legion of devils that Jesus set free at Gadarene, this man regained his right mind and began to praise God. He whom the Son has made free is free indeed! I believe Jesus is the same today as then. We must always give God the glory in everything we do. He alone deserves it. For the rest of my life on earth, I want to do those things that will glorify Him for He alone is worthy. I want to please my heavenly Father in such a way that someday I will hear him say "Well done, my child, enter into the joys of the Lord."

Through the years of being led by the Spirit, it has taken my wife and I to places others would not go. We did not go for the money. But we would go to lift up Jesus and see the poor and needy blessed. And we were blessed to see the blind healed, the deaf and dumb hear and speak, the lame leap for joy, and the altars filled with people weeping before the Lord asking forgiveness for their sins. What joy it brought to our hearts to give Him all the glory! He alone is worthy!

God has blessed me with wonderful children. Each one is anointed of God and filled with the Holy Spirit. It is such a joy to my heart to see them growing stronger in the Lord as they serve Him daily. And I thank God for the anointing He bestowed upon them from birth. I am a mighty blessed man to have a wonderful wife like I do and a family serving God by my side. I thank God and give Him all the glory for such a wonderful life and for His agapé love. I am so grateful to Him for His mercy and His grace. I believe it is the Father's will for all His children to have the best in life. I believe He will give us all He can trust us with. We must never take God for granted and we must look to Him as the All-Supreme.

In my study of the Word, I have found God to be more than just the Author of all creation. I have found Him to be my Lord and my God. I have found Him to be my Savior and my Healer. He is my Father and I am His child. I have been begotten of Him. I have fellowship with Him as a son with his father.

When we are born-again, the Holy Spirit will reveal to us the depth of love the Father has for His children. I am not an adopted child, although I call Him Abba Father. Children are adopted because someone loves them but they are different from those who are born into a family. God chose me before the foundation of the world and, therefore, I am begotten of Him. I believe each of us was born for a purpose. We have a vocation set out by God; a path He has chosen for us to follow even if we choose not to follow that path.

"I therefore, the prisoner of the Lord, beseech you that ye walk worthy of the vocation wherewith ye are called, With all lowliness and meekness, with longsuffering, forbearing one another in love; Endeavoring to keep the unity of the Spirit in the bond of peace. There is one body, and one Spirit, even as ye are called in one hope of your calling; One Lord, one faith, one baptism, One God and Father of all, who is above all, and through all, and in you all."

- **EPHESIANS 4:1-6**

This scripture tells me I was born for a purpose. It tells me my Father loves me and I love Him.

God will be in our tomorrows, planning and making provisions for us. That is why He said, "Take no thought for tomorrow." He wants us to know He is taking care of everything if we will only trust Him. God was in our yesterday because He made provision for these blessings in the past. He chose us to be begotten of Him from the foundation of the world. And it was through the sacrifice of His only begotten Son on the cross at Calvary that paved a way for us. God is in our today because He is there when we need Him. We can call on Him day or night in the name of Jesus. He is a present help in the time of trouble. He is kind and compassionate to those who love Him with all their heart, soul, body, and strength. And He blesses us with all spiritual blessings.

When Jesus sent His disciples out, they returned and told Him all they had done in His name. He listened to them and then He told them to take a vacation and rest. Jesus wants us to give a report to Him about what we are doing for the Father although He already knows all about it. I believe He enjoys it when we tell Him. I believe He is proud when we bring Him a good report and not a bad one.

Our heavenly Father gives us jobs to do just like our earthly parents did. When I grew up on the farm, my dad would have me to plow the field or chop wood or feed the livestock. Whatever work it was, when I would finish the job and tell him I was done, he would smile or maybe pat me on the shoulder. I knew he was proud of me. Sometimes, if we had been working hard, he would say, "You can take tomorrow off and go fishing." He knew I needed a break. I loved my dad and mom and I know they loved me and all my brothers and sisters. And I know my heavenly Father loves me and I love Him.

As the Holy Spirit guides us, He always teaches us to do good even to those who despitefully use or abuse us. I could not have made this journey alone or without Him holding my hand. In every battle of life He has been there with me to lead me to victory. To Him be all the glory forever and ever. My heavenly Father has given me everything in this life that I have needed. Since I have come to this revelation knowledge, there is never a day that my inner man doesn't praise Him and give Him glory with all that is within me. When my natural man is facing storms and I have grown tired and weary on the journey, I will still praise him because I owe Him my all. He gave His all for me and I can do no less for Him. I would like to say right now, "Thank You Lord, for your blessings on me!"

Why don't you try it yourself? It will make you feel good.

"A merry heart doeth good like a medicine: but a broken spirit drieth the bones."

- **PROVERBS 17:22**

"A merry heart maketh a cheerful countenance: but by sorrow of the heart the spirit is broken."

- **PROVERBS 15:13**

Let heaven and earth praise His holy name and give Him glory!